Pride or Praise?

by

Kenneth A. Penman, Ph.D.

XULON PRESS

Xulon Press
11350 Random Hills Road
Suite 800
Fairfax, VA 22030
(703) 279-6511
XulonPress.com

To order additional copies, call 1-866-909-BOOK (2665).

Illustrations by Karen Hornfelt

Table of Contents

Acknowledgements

My heartfelt thanks to my wife Pat, without whose loving support and secretarial skills this book would not have been created. I also wish to thank several friends who read the manuscript and gave helpful suggestions. A special thanks to Karen Hornfelt, whose tremendous artistic talent helped make the topic a little lighter, and most of all praise to our loving Father, the living God who gives us all knowledge and power to do His will.

—Ken Penman

Introduction

Unfortunately, too often man excessively indulges in self-esteem. We stand ready and waiting to take credit for our many accomplishments, forgetting who makes it all possible. Can't you imagine God observing this prideful world and thinking, it has been over 7000 years, and they still don't get the message.

Webster defines pride as: "a) an overhigh opinion of oneself; exaggerated self-esteem; conceit; b) haughty behavior resulting from this; arrogance". This is the attitude being addressed in this treatise and should not be confused with the joy, or happiness, we experience when good things happen.

Pride is a component of our personalities with which we all have to deal. Christians, particularly, need to examine and control their pride based on the teaching of God's word.

One might ask the question: By accepting the teaching "Blessed are the meek . . ." (Matthew 5:5), is it really necessary to be so humble that we allow people to take advantage of us? It may well be, if it is to God's glory. However, we seldom see anyone making that sacrifice. On the other hand, nearly every day we associate with people who are so "puffed up" with what they perceive to be their own importance that it is often difficult to tolerate them. Realistically, all of us fall between those two extremes; that is, have a certain amount of pride in some aspect of our lives. This pride could be in our accomplishments, our children, our possessions, our country, our appearance, and so on. The natural questions to ask, then, are: Is pride really wrong? Isn't a little pride good for one's self-confidence? Is it, then, a matter of the amount of pride one has as to whether it is good or bad? As in all other aspects of life, the Bible has a great deal to say about pride. The Old and New Testaments abound with examples of how men and women dealt with pride, of what God thinks of human pride, the source of pride, and how we ought to deal with pride in our daily lives. In addition, the scriptures also have a great deal to say about concepts that are closely interrelated with pride such as vanity, arrogance, haughtiness, humility, boasting, glory, confidence, assurance, AND praise!

Secular psychology, of course, also has a good deal to say about pride. Many secular psychology books deal with how one can be at complete peace with one's self—even if you are so full of pride that no one can stand to be around you. Humanistic psychology seems to condemn any restraints upon the individual will and, therefore, "it's OK for me to be prideful, if I really deserve to be because of my great talents or accomplishments! A very famous American architect has been quoted as saying: "Early in life I had to choose between honest arrogance and hypocritical humility. I chose honest arrogance and have seen no occasion to change". This quotation is representative of man's way of thinking. Frequently the Biblical teaching on a particular aspect of life does not agree with man's view on the subject and this is precisely the case when studying about pride. Reference to secular psychology in this book, then, will only be made to give examples of what man is being taught today about concepts related to the idea of pride. These "modern" ideas may seem good to the ears of the reader; because, in many cases, they are what we want to hear. We generally do not want to hear teachings that we instinctively reject, based upon our own feelings! The classic secular writing on the subject of pride is Jane Austen's novel *Pride and Prejudice*. Even though it was first published in 1813, it still remains a literary classic. Innumerable critiques have been written on this literary piece, and many analyses have been made of Mr. Darcy's pride. In fact, throughout the book Jane Austen discusses philosophically the positive and negative aspects of this central character's pride in a humanistic framework. Few Christian writers have dealt with this topic in recent years.

The primary reference for the theme of this book will be the Holy Scriptures. Examples will be given from the scriptures, and application of those principles will be made to illustrate how we ought to live today according to God's Word. References to the scriptures used are taken from the New International Version of the Bible.

It would seem important that a Christian book, dealing with any subject, consider what God says about the topic. What is God's view of Pride? What is the source of pride? Why are so many people burdened with such a need to hold themselves in high esteem? Isn't a little pride OK if it is controlled? Although these initial chapters may seem somewhat academic, it is imperative that the basic material covered in them is known for a good appreciation of the material that follows. After these initial Chapters we will look at pride as it relates to possession of material things, relationship to prominent people, pride in country, spiritual pride, and so on.

As you read this book, I hope you will examine pride in your own life. Do we really give God the glory He deserves?

CHAPTER 1

The Source of Human Pride

The Bible clearly explains for us where pride originated. There was, at the beginning of time, a host of beings that were created by God and called angels (Psalms 148). Actually, the word angel designates an office, rather than describing a person. That office is associated with the heavenly service of being a messenger. So God created these heavenly beings, whose function was primarily to act as messengers. In addition, we know several other facts about these beings. Christ, although He was taught of the Spirit and filled with the Spirit, was fed, defended, and strengthened by angels. Since angels are created heavenly beings, they do not reproduce or die. We are told in Luke 20:36 that after the resurrection we will no longer die for we will be like angels. Ezekiel describes angels as having wisdom and other traits that resemble human personality. Angels are also described as having splendor and beauty, which leads us to believe that they have some kind of recognizable form.

One of these angels, called Lucifer, was anointed by God to be a guardian cherub. Lucifer was blameless from the day he was created. He was a model of perfection, full of wisdom and perfect in beauty. We know Lucifer was in Eden and existed in great splendor (Ezekiel 28:13), so it may have been that God had assigned Lucifer to act as guardian and chief messenger on the earth He had created. It seems, from the account in Ezekiel, that Lucifer had not yet fallen; because we also read in Genesis 1:31 that God finished creation of the earth, including man, assigned a guardian angel, and declared that ALL was very good. We also know, from the account in Genesis 3, that Satan tempted man and he subsequently fell into a state of sin. Therefore, it may well be that it was sometime between Genesis 1 and 3 that Lucifer rebelled.

We can only imagine the thoughts Lucifer had just prior to his rebellion. Here he was in a fantastically beautiful earth and he was the guardian cherub over all of it. He was also a model of perfection, full of wisdom and perfect in beauty. He saw man, whom God had also created to be perfect, and he was to be in limited control over all this! Everything looked so great for Lucifer except for one thing —he was still SUBORDINATE to God! So Lucifer began to think that since he had so much power and was so great and beautiful he didn't want to be subordinate to anyone—even to his creator; and, therefore, CHOSE to attempt to become equal with God (Isaiah 14:12-15). Lucifer had no downward pull to encourage him in these evil thoughts. There was apparently no one around to deceive him into doing wrong. Lucifer chose to do wrong with full knowledge of what he was doing because of his pride. Lucifer became so self-centered, believing that he didn't need God, that he attempted to gain a place equal to God in heaven. Lucifer said: "I will ascend to heaven; I will raise my throne about the stars of God; I will sit enthroned on the mount of assembly, on the utmost heights of the sacred mountain. I will ascend above the tops of the clouds; I will make myself like the Most High" (Isaiah 14:13-14). Wow! Can you imagine yourself saying that to God! It would take a very rebellious, angry, over-confident person to even think of saying such a thing!

We read, then, of the ensuing war in heaven in Revelation 12:7-9. "And there was war in heaven. Michael and his angels fought against the dragon, and the dragon and his angels fought back. But he was not strong enough, and they lost their place in heaven. The great dragon was hurled down—that ancient serpent called the devil, or Satan, who leads the whole world astray. He was hurled to the earth, and his angels with him. Prior to his fall, Lucifer was called the morning star and often in the scriptures angels are referred to as stars. We read in Revelation 12:4 that "His (Satan's) tail swept a third of the stars out of the sky and flung them to the earth. So Satan and one third of all the heavenly angels rebelled and were cast out of heaven to earth, where Satan's battle with God continues even to this day as he desires to win us over to his side. Jesus was an eyewitness to Lucifer's fall. He says in Luke (10:18) "I saw Satan fall like lightning from heaven". It was after the fall that God changed Lucifer's name to Satan, Devil, and/or Apollyon.

Therefore, if we believe the scriptures, including what our Lord said about angels in general and Lucifer specifically, we cannot escape the fact that 1) Satan was, at one time, a beautiful creature, 2) that because of his self-centeredness and pride he chose to oppose God, and 3) he was thrown out of heaven. He was not destroyed at that time. He is, indeed, alive and well on earth. He and his host of angels have a great deal of influence on people today. Understanding the FACT of Satan's existence and the FACT that he has a great influence on men is paramount to the study of pride. If pride could bring about the fall of one of God's most beautiful and wise angels, it most certainly can bring down mortal man. So this is our world-a society which is greatly influenced and guided by satanic value judgments and is also guided by satanic pride. It is no wonder, then, that humanistic philosophies are so readily accepted by much of humankind.

"How you have fallen from heaven, O morning star, Son of
the dawn! You have been cast down to the Earth,
you who once laid low the nations!"
Isaiah 14:12

The "I can do it, I don't need any help, and who needs God", attitudes are precisely the same prideful attitudes that Lucifer had. In Isaiah 14, Satan says: "I WILL ascend to heaven, I WILL raise my throne above the stars of God, I WILL sit enthroned on the mount of assembly, I WILL ascend above the tips of the clouds, and I WILL make myself like the Most High". Satan had such an inflated ego that his classic five I WILLs were indicative of the desire in his heart to be equal with God. The "I WILL" spirit is the spirit of rebellion. The "I, I, I" mentality does not glorify God; rather, it glorifies self! We once received some literature from a prominent television evangelist. In the two-page paper the name of Jesus Christ was mentioned twice. The personal pronoun "I", referring to the evangelist, was used thirty-seven times! Satan must be especially pleased when he influences those who preach the Gospel. Pride prevents man from coming to know God because, in order to accept God, man has to accept the fact that he is inferior to his creator! This is very difficult for many people to do. In fact, it was so difficult for Lucifer to handle that he chose to rebel and lost.

"Alright", you say, "even if the fall of Lucifer was the origin of pride, what does this have to do with me? I am a Christian and am free from the kingdom of Satan! The devil can't touch me!" WRONG! Nothing could be further from the truth. It is true that the devil can never completely defeat a Christian, but the devil can certainly demoralize and tremendously influence a Christian. If Satan did not oppose the Spirit of God, every Christian would be a powerful force to destroy his kingdom of darkness. In fact, Satan and his army of fallen angels must work "overtime" on Christians. Satan has been, and is currently, very successful in influencing non-Christians. He is not concerned about them, because they are already "on his side"! However, because of the protection of God's angels and the indwelling of the Holy Spirit in the Christian's life, Satan must expend most of his effort trying to disrupt the life of the Christian. That's why Paul spent so much time explaining the importance of the Christian putting on the whole armor of God so that we can take a stand against the devil's schemes (Ephesians 6:11). We need that protection against the powerful force of Satan.

Throughout the scriptures, Satan is charged with four primary sins. He is the "father of lying, murder, malice, and pride. Because Satan is still actively opposing God, he is also trying to defeat those whom God created, and especially those who have decided to live according to God's law. Satan is continually trying to increase his army to oppose God. He is not satisfied with one third of the host of angels, he also wants to lead as many humans astray as he can, so that they will not "be with God". Since we are essentially sensuous human beings, Satan often works through an appeal of pleasure. Through our emotions, he works on and exploits our fears; and through our intellect, or mind, he makes his appeal to pride. Paul teaches us in Ephesians 6:12 that our struggle is not against flesh and blood, but against the rulers, against the authorities, against the powers of this dark world and against the spiritual forces of evil in the heavenly realms. This is where it becomes difficult for us as Christians, because we can sensually see, feel, observe, and enjoy benefits of worldly pleasures; but what Paul is telling us is that it is the spiritual, or that which is unseen, that is important. Paul tells us in Colossians 2:18 that we should not let anyone who delights in false humility and the worship of angels to disqualify us from "the prize". Essentially, Paul is telling us that 1) false humility is another way of describing pride, 2) that this pride comes from Satan for deceptive purposes, 3) that by dwelling in pride or false humility we are in a sense worshipping an angel, and 4) that we should not worship angels. Who is the fallen angel? Who is the father of pride? SATAN! Unfortunately, there are many cults in the world today that believe in and actually worship Satan.

In 1 John 3:8-12 we read what Christ said about Satan and where he stood in relation to the sin of pride. "He who does what is sinful is of the devil, because the devil has been sinning from the beginning." In the beginning Satan was so prideful that he wanted to be equal with God. In fact the very reason the Son of God came to us on earth in human form was to destroy the devil's work. So Christ appeared on earth to show mankind why pride is the forerunner to destruction. During Christ's ministry, He was preaching to the multitude near the lake. After Jesus told the crowd the Parable of the Weeds, He and the disciples went into a house and the disciples asked Christ to explain the parable to them more fully. He answered: "The one who sowed the good seed is the Son of Man. The field is the world, and the good seed stands for the sons of the kingdom. The weeds are the sons of the evil one, and the enemy who sows them is the devil . . ." (Matthew 13:37-39). So, in this context, Christ is the source of the good seed, humility, but it is Satan who is planting the seed of pride in the hearts of men of the world. In another case, when Christ was involved in the beginning of His "trial", Jesus called the Jews, who were not accepting Him for who He claimed to be, stubborn and prideful; saying they belonged to their father, the devil, and that they wanted to carry out their father's desire (John 8:44). The Jews were convinced then, as they are today, that the messiah did not and will not return to earth until He comes as their deliverer.

There are several additional important references in the Bible that give us knowledge of the fact that pride is, in fact, of the devil. In James 3:14-15 we read about how there is a worldly wisdom that is opposed to heavenly wisdom. "But if you harbor bitter envy and selfish ambition in your hearts, do not boast about it or deny the truth. Such "wisdom" does not come down from heaven but is earthly, unspiritual, of the devil". Worldly wisdom tells us that it is good to have pride in what you do and that there is nothing wrong with taking pride in your accomplishments! Heavenly wisdom says give all glory to the creator who made it possible for you to do a good job. Can you see a difference between being satisfied with doing the best you can in all endeavors of life with what God has given to you, and praising Him for it, compared to being proud that you have done such a good job all on your own? Paul shows how Satan appears as an angel of light to deceive us on matters such as this when he is describing false apostles to the Corinthians: "For such men are false apostles, deceitful workmen, masquerading as apostles of Christ". And no wonder, for Satan himself masquerades as an angel of light. It is not surprising, then, if his servants masquerade as servants of righteousness. The world rulers of present darkness are headed by the Devil, whom we have previously seen is a fallen angel with power and cunning cleverness, against whom Christians are called on to wrestle with daily. This is not the claim of an isolated passage of the Word. It is the teaching of the Bible from Genesis to Revelation. Satan would indeed like very much to convince us that pride is OK (2 Corinthians 11:13-15). Paul gave us another example of the place of pride and the fate of the prideful in 1 Timothy 3:6 when he is explaining the qualifications of overseers and deacons of the church: "He must not be a recent convert, or he may become conceited and fall under the same judgment as the devil." Paul knew Satan tempts by pride and that a person in a leadership position can easily become inflated with a prideful spirit. He then tells us of the fate of that person.

There is no doubt about the ultimate fate of Satan. John, in Revelation 20:2-10, gives a vivid account of Satan's ultimate doom. We all have resisted the temptation of the devil at some time in the past. It is possible to resist him at the present, if we so choose, and we will be able to resist him in the future. Therefore, we have in our grasp the power to choose or reject being prideful. As Christians, we are to submit ourselves to God. We are to resist the devil in all ways, and he will flee from us. We are commanded to resist him as the tempter of pride (James 4:7). We also know that no temptation has ever overtaken us that is not common to man.

Coming to grips with pride has always been, and always will be, a problem for all of mankind. There is no doubt, then, what the source of pride is according to the Word of God. We know the source of pride, and we also know our source for all things as Christians; and we know that we can resist the temptation to be prideful with the help of the Holy Spirit.

FATHER, HELP US TO RECOGNIZE THAT THE SOURCE OF PRIDE IS SATAN. WHEN WE BECOME PRIDEFUL WE TEND TO ELEVATE OURSELVES TO A PLACE OF HIGH ESTEEM THAT WE DON'T DESERVE. WE KNOW SATAN WOULD LIKE US TO BECOME FILLED WITH PRIDE BECAUSE HE WOULD HAVE SUCCEEDED IN GETTING US TO BE ON HIS SIDE. FATHER, HELP US TO BECOME HUMBLE, TO RECOGNIZE THAT YOU ARE OUR SOURCE, THAT WE CAN DO NOTHING APART FROM YOU, OUR SOURCE, AND THAT ALL GLORY SHOULD BE GIVEN TO YOU. AMEN

CHAPTER 2

God's View of Pride

If we are going to examine the Biblical view of man's pride, it seems logical to look at the Word as it relates to what God says about pride. Does He condone it? Does He encourage it? Does He like it? Does He say it is a matter of degree? Does He dislike it, or does He hate it?

You are probably now saying, "Wait a minute, anyone knows that a little pride is OK! As long as one is not prideful in excess it surely can't be that sinful! After all, everyone has a little pride. In fact, shouldn't we all have a little pride in order to maintain our self-esteem, self-confidence, and self-respect!" Another way we might try to rationalize, or justify, that pride is OK from God's view is to say that, probably, in the Greek and Hebrew languages, the meaning for the word was different; and that pride, as we define it today, must be acceptable to God. Sorry, that is just not true. "Well!" you say, "Didn't God create all things, including pride; therefore, if he made it, isn't a little of His "creation" in our personality alright?" We answered that question in the first chapter; and the answer is NO, based on the fate of Lucifer. In a later chapter we will also look at what God expects from us in the way of doing our best at anything and then feeling confident that we have done our best for God.

If we examine the scriptures thoroughly, we find that God does indeed hate certain things. It is surprising to many people to discover that a God of love would, or even could, hate anything. The scriptures say that God hates the deeds of faithless men. He hates the wrong paths man chooses to take. He hates double-minded people (that is, people who are hypocrites). He hates falsehood. He hates robbery and iniquity. He hates divorce. He hates those who cling to false idols. And, yes, He also hates PRIDE AND ARROGANCE. In Proverbs 6:17 we read that there are six things the Lord hates, seven that are detestable to him: haughty eyes (haughtiness is another word for being prideful), a lying tongue, hands that shed innocent blood, a heart that devises wicked schemes, feet that are quick to rush into evil, a false witness who pours out lies, and a man who stirs up dissension among brothers. Also, in Proverbs 8:13, the Lord, through Solomon, comes right out and says that HE HATES PRIDE AND ARROGANCE! In addition to the use of that strong word HATE, pride is also described as something that God DETESTS, or STRONGLY DISLIKES. God also abhors and opposes the proud. After reviewing the references in God's Word that describe what He thinks of pride, it is rather difficult to rationalize the idea that God, in any way, shape, or form, condones pride in our lives.

In the book of Romans, we read how men have become gossips, slanderers, god-haters, insolent, arrogant and boastful (Romans 1:30). On numerous other occasions in the Bible, God tells us that He dislikes pride so much that He will not listen to the petitions of the haughty and will eventually put an end to the arrogance of the haughty (i.e. Job 35:12 and Daniel 10:12). Do you know of any Christians who are prideful and have trouble experiencing the power of prayer? Possibly it is because of their arrogance that God does not listen to their petitions! These are very strong indictments against being prideful!

**". . . God opposes the proud but gives grace to the humble."
James 4:6**

Pride, according to modern dictionaries, is defined as a psychological trait held by a person who holds a high or inordinate opinion of his own importance, merit, or superiority. This inflated image can be cherished in the mind alone, or in addition, be displayed in the way we conduct ourselves outwardly. Pride is a lofty and often arrogant assumption of one's superiority in some area of life. When one is openly prideful, others are usually left with the impression that the prideful individual claims sole credit for the accomplishment and perceived superiority. Conceit is a closely related term to pride and also implies an exaggerated estimate of one's own abilities or attainments. Self-esteem implies an estimate of oneself that is more complimentary than that held by others, and vanity implies self-admiration and an excessive desire to be admired by others. We will examine all these concepts and attempt to understand what God's Word says about them in subsequent chapters of this book. The antonym of these terms is, of course, humility. A humble person is modest, meek, does not place himself above others in importance, and is quick to give his creator the glory.

When Peter was writing to God's elect in various cities he said: "Young men ... Clothe yourselves with humility toward one another, because God opposes the proud BUT GIVES GRACE TO THE HUMBLE." That is the key to the whole theme of this book! God indeed does hate pride and even opposes the proud, BUT He gives grace to the humble. Think of it! He does not want us to be proud, and if we do refrain from being prideful, He gives us grace (the free and unmerited favor and love bestowed upon us by God); and, if we have God's grace, why do we need to be proud! God wants our hearts; and, if our grace and peace is in Him, why do we need to be patted on the head like a puppy or express our pride to other people! If a person's heart is right with God, he/she doesn't need pride. If, on the other hand, our hearts are filled with greed, malice, deceit, envy, slander, arrogance, folly, and we have haughty eyes, we are, in fact, dwelling in sin. In Proverbs 21:4 we read that haughty eyes and a proud heart, the lamp of the wicked, are sin. God also shows us in Isaiah 66:2 that the one who is humble and contrite in spirit and trembles at His Word is the one whom He honors. Also, in Psalms 149:4 we read that the Lord takes delight in his people; He crowns the humble with salvation. Did you ever think about why so many people refuse to make that final decision to accept Christ as their Lord and Savior? That is a humbling decision and is very difficult to do for a proud person!

Throughout history, God has reacted against the proud. Refusing to acknowledge the fact that God abhors pride does not go without a consequence. Going back in history about 3700 years, an interesting contrast is seen, which illustrates this point, in the case of Moses and his confrontations with Pharaoh regarding letting the Israelites leave Egypt. Moses was a very humble man; in fact, we are told in Numbers 12:3 that Moses was more humble than anyone else on the face of the earth, and this may very well be the reason why God used Moses as He did. Anyway, Moses and his brother Aaron went to Pharaoh (who was a very proud ruler) and said to him, "This is what the Lord, the God of the Hebrews, says: "How long will you refuse to humble yourself before me?" Pharaoh was so filled with pride because of his status and power that no Hebrew God was going to tell him what to do! It was not until Eqypt endured many plagues and lost all its firstborn that Pharaoh finally said they could go. Later the Israelites themselves, after many years of wandering in the desert, became very proud and independent people and strayed from God's commands. The Lord spoke to Moses on Mount Sinai and said that He would punish the Israelites if they did not listen to Him (Leviticus 26:19), "I will break down your stubborn pride and make the sky above you like iron and the ground beneath you like bronze." God was angry with the Israelites because of their feeling of self-sufficiency.

About 585 BC the political leaders in Jerusalem thought they were safe within the fortification of Jerusalem; but through Ezekiel 7:24-27, the Lord said: "I will put an end to this pride of the mighty, and their sanctuaries will be desecrated . . . then they will know I am Lord." The Moabites who were geographically located just East of the Dead Sea, were known for their extreme pride, and God said that Moab would become like Sodom. "This is what they will get in return for their pride, for insulting and mocking the people of the Lord Almighty" (Zephaniah 2:10-11). Sodom, in addition to many other sins, was filled with arrogance, haughtiness, and pride; and God completely destroyed Sodom (Sodom was located South of Jerusalem). In Isaiah 10:12 we read where the Lord says: "I will punish the king of Assyria for the willful pride of his heart and the haughty look of his eyes." Isaiah also prophesies about the fate of Tyre, who will be responsible for that fate, and why the punishment will be inflicted in 23:9 – "The Lord Almighty planned it, to bring low the pride of all glory and to humble all who are renowned on the earth."

So Jerusalem and all the nations around Jerusalem to the North, East, South, and West were proud and were subsequently punished because of their pride. In Isaiah the Lord says "I will punish the world for its evil, the wicked for their sins. I will put an end to the arrogance of the haughty and will humble the pride of the ruthless." Repeatedly we read in the scriptures that God sustains the humble and will bring low the pride of men.

So God hates pride so much that He has in the past, and will in the future, inflict punishment on individuals and nations who are so prideful and arrogant that they think their ways are sufficient. Yet, today secular humanism is leading us as a nation, and as individuals, down the exact same prideful path to destruction.

One might ask, "Why does God hate pride so much?" The answer seems quite simple. God wants our dependence to be on HIM—not ourselves. Today, it is very "in" to be self-sufficient, to be very confident of oneself, and this gets at the very heart of pride. If we possess a very prideful nature and gloat over our own attributes, accomplishments and/or acquisitions, we are not relying on, or giving God credit for anything. With the tremendous influence of secular humanism on the lives of people today, we are constantly being led to believe that we (man) can do it—we can do anything. The fate of man is in the hands of man and who needs God! In fact, humanistic thinking denies the existence of God and indeed deifies man. Can you imagine how distasteful this must be to our creator! Today He must be looking down at us as individuals and as a nation and thinking "here they go again, rejecting their creator and thinking they can do everything on their own. Hasn't history taught them anything?" Consider how our national leaders are criticized by a certain segment of our fellow Americans each time one of them invokes the name of "God".

Several proverbs also instruct us on pride. When pride comes, then comes disgrace, BUT with humility comes wisdom (Proverbs 11:2). "Pride only breeds quarrels, but wisdom is found in those who take advice" (Proverbs 13:10). "Pride goes before destruction, a haughty spirit before a fall" (Proverbs 16:18). It's no wonder, then, that God opposes the proud. The more prideful we become, the less dependent we become on Him. But God gives grace to the humble, and His grace should be sufficient for the life of the Christian. We can also learn a lot from what the Lord told Daniel in a vision: "Do not be afraid, Daniel. Since the first day that you set your mind to gain understanding and to humble yourself before your God, your words were heard, . . ." (Daniel 10:12).

This whole concept is often difficult for many Christians to accept, because they see prideful non-Christians being very successful in all kinds of endeavors—in business, in health, in personal relations, and so on. They see nonbelievers who are wicked, arrogant, and prideful, prospering and seeming to have few struggles. The wicked seem to be free of the burdens of most men and often sneer at God's laws and speak with malice against God's people. We wonder why they are so successful when pride seems to be their necklace; and, at the same time, many Christians, some of whom are very humble, have all kinds of problems! The Psalmist has a response to this (73:16-17), "When I tried to understand all this, it was oppressive to me till I entered the sanctuary of God; then I understood their final destiny." So, it may appear that the wicked are having a much better life at the present; and they may, in fact, be having a better life, according to today's "worldly standards", BUT we know God will deal with the proud and the wicked, and our status in eternity is much more important than our status on earth. Remember, God never promised us, as Christians, that we would not have problems. Character is primarily developed by learning to confront and deal with problems. However, He did promise to be with us in all our trials and tribulations.

FATHER, BY EXAMINING YOUR WORD WE HAVE NO CHOICE BUT TO ACCEPT THE FACT THAT YOU HATE PRIDE. WE KNOW, LORD, THAT YOU WANT OUR HEARTS; AND, WHEN WE DWELL IN PRIDE AND EXTREME SELF-CONFIDENCE, WE BEGIN TO BELIEVE WE DON'T NEED YOU. FORGIVE US, FATHER, FOR OUR PRIDE. FILL US WITH YOUR GRACE, SO THAT WE WILL HAVE NO ROOM FOR A PRIDEFUL HEART. IN JESUS' NAME. AMEN

CHAPTER 3

Isn't a Little Pride Good?

The first two chapters of this book may seem to have been quite "heavy". After all, if one accepts the scriptural teachings included in those chapters, what is there left to say? Pride is sin! It is an absolute! God hates pride, and Satan is the source of pride! There is no way one can rationalize the fact that even a little personal pride can be good! Even in the secular world the word "boasting" depicts an unpleasant act to many people. There is, however, a subtle difference in pride, per se, and what specifically one is boasting about. Boasting is actually a manifestation of what comes out of the heart by way of our speech. It does, indeed, reflect our inner thoughts; and the boast could be based on personal pride, or on our confidence in knowing some fact (i.e. salvation), or in knowing God. This declaration, or boast, is not (at least it should not be) intended to make us feel inwardly greater than others, or to attempt to have others look at us as being superior (i.e. vanity). Rather, we boast about things of the Lord because of our deep confidence, or faith. Jeremiah and Paul warn us to be careful when we boast, even of the Lord, because people will often misinterpret our hearts and think we are conceited. We should not boast, but if we must boast, we should boast in the Lord. If a person is being prideful about something they have done, and believe they deserve all the credit for that achievement, that is, indeed, sin, because it leaves God completely out of the picture.

The scriptures are very clear in differentiating between those things about which we should boast and those things about which we are not to boast. Both the Old and New Testaments condemn boasting and being prideful about our own accomplishments. It is impossible to verify, by using the scriptures, that the human trait of being proud of <u>our</u> accomplishments is good. <u>Scriptures only condone boasting if it is directed to our Lord.</u>

How often have you gone about your daily tasks boasting about and praising the Lord? When was the last time you boasted to someone about a brother or sister "doing well in the Lord"? When was the last time you joined with other believers in boasting about what God is doing in the world today? When was the last time you boasted about the fact that you know the Lord Jesus Christ in a personal way? When was the last time you proudly and publicly expressed your belief that Christ arose from the dead and is alive today? And on the other side of the picture, how long ago was it that you last boasted about some accomplishment <u>you</u> made, or about what a clever thing <u>your</u> child did, or about some possession <u>you</u> have, or about what a good decision <u>you</u> just made, or about how strong <u>you</u> are? Of course, Christians can become obnoxious and cause people around them to "be turned off" if their boasting in the Lord is not done in a tactful way. We are told by Peter that we should always be ready to give the reason for our hope in a gentle and respectful manner (1 Peter 3:15-16). If boasting in the Lord is not done carefully, one can fall into the trap of "spiritual pride". We will discuss that more fully in a later chapter.

The apostle Paul teaches us a great deal about pride. In nearly every letter he wrote he addressed this problem. Yet, he has also been improperly accused of being prideful himself. This criticism has been primarily directed at his statement in 2 Corinthians 12:6. "Even if I should choose to boast, I would not be a fool, because I would be speaking the truth . . ." This, upon superficial examination, may lead one to believe that Paul was indeed a prideful person. Even if he were to be prideful to a degree, it would not contradict the numerous teachings he gave us in his writings—it would only prove his humanness! We will examine Paul's teaching on pride later, but first let's take a look at some Old Testament references that address boasting and the things about which we should be boasting. There are two beautiful Psalms that suggest what we should boast about. In Psalm 34:1-3, David wrote: "I will extol the Lord at all times; His praise will always be on my lips. My soul will boast in the Lord; let the afflicted hear and rejoice. Glorify the Lord with me; let us exalt His name together." And in Psalm 44:8, the Sons of Korah wrote: "In God we make our boast all day long, and we will praise your name forever." If we were predisposed to praise God and boast of God "all day long", what a difference it would make in our daily walk! This boasting does not necessarily have to be an outward verbal expression—although there would not be anything wrong with this, if it were done in a loving way; but it can also be done inwardly (in the depths of our soul) as a constant reminder of just who our source really is! So, if we are continually praising God, exalting Him, and giving Him the glory He rightly deserves, we are, as the Psalmist says, "boasting in our souls of the Lord", and that is OK.

Probably the most beautiful teaching about pride found in the Old Testament is the message the Lord gave to the prophet Jeremiah. This is what the Lord said: "Let not the wise man boast of his wisdom, or the strong man boast of his strength, or the rich man boast of his riches, but let him who boasts boast about this: that he understands and knows me, that I am the Lord, who exercises kindness, justice and

"Now Moses was a very humble man, more humble than
anyone else on the face of the earth."
Numbers 12:3

righteousness on earth, for in these I delight."(Jeremiah 9:23-24) Notice the wording in the middle phrase "but let him who boasts boast about this". The Lord is really saying He doesn't want us to boast at all; but, if you find it necessary in your humanness to boast about something, boast about this—that you know me; but do not boast about yourself! What a blessing and comfort it is to know that we have a personal Lord and Savior. If we must boast, we should boast in this fact. The writer of Hebrews adds another thing that we can boast about: "But Christ is faithful as a son over God's house. And we are His house, if we hold on to our courage and the hope of which we boast." (Hebrews 3:6) So the hope and assurance that one day we will be with God in His kingdom is also something about which we should boast, if we are so inclined. Paul's teachings about pride are well rooted in the Old Testament, as well as in personal revelation. Paul makes his position on pride very clear in Galatians 6:14, where he says: "May I never boast except in the cross of our Lord Jesus Christ"; in 1 Corinthians 1:31: "Therefore, as it is written: Let him who boasts boast in the Lord"; and in 2 Corinthians 10:17: "But, let him who boasts boast in the Lord."

Paul, on numerous occasions, speaks of pride and boasting in relation to the "brotherhood of Christ". When Paul was writing to the Corinthians he said: "I have great confidence in you; I take great pride in you. I am greatly encouraged; in all our troubles my joy knows no bounds." (2 Corinthians 7:4) Paul had sent Titus to the Corinthians, and Titus' spirit was refreshed by being with the believers in Corinth. Paul says in verse 14: "I had boasted to him (Titus) about you, and you have not embarrassed me." So Paul was proud that the Corinthians had received Titus well, as Paul had convinced him they would. Again, in 2 Corinthians 8:24, Paul says: "Therefore show these men (Titus and the brothers accompanying him) the proof of your love and the reason for our pride in you, so that the churches can see it." So the people in God's family should be able to see one another taking pride in the things of God! In Paul's second letter to the Thessalonians, he begins with thanksgiving for them as brothers who are keeping the faith: "We ought always to thank God for you, brothers, and rightly so, because your faith is growing more and more, and the love every one of you has for each other is increasing. Therefore, among God's churches we boast about our perseverance and faith in all the persecutions and trials you are enduring." (2 Thessalonians 1:3-4)

Paul alludes to boasting and pride to a greater extent in 2 Corinthians than in any other epistle. We notice several additional references to pride in the "brotherhood" in the earlier chapters, and a defense of his "apparent pride" in chapters 11 through 13. In several places in the epistle, Paul is attempting to explain how this mutual praise or confidence in believers should be exemplified. "Now this is our boast: Our conscience testifies that we have conducted ourselves in the world, and especially in our relations with you, in the holiness and sincerity that are from God. We have done so, not according to worldly wisdom, but according to God's grace." (2 Corinthians 1:12) Then, in verse 14, he says: "As you have understood us in part, you will come to understand fully that you can boast of us just as we will boast of you in the day of the Lord Jesus." In 5:14 Paul adds a very important distinction between the things mortal man sees as worthy of pride compared to what the believer sees as Heavenly wisdom: "We are not trying to commend ourselves to you again, but are giving you an opportunity to take pride in us, so that you can answer those who take pride in what is seen rather than what is in the heart." So much of Paul's boasting was about the steadfast faith of individuals and of various churches for the purpose of <u>edification of the</u> <u>"body of Christ"</u>. "For even if I boast somewhat freely about the authority the Lord gave us for building you up rather than pulling you down, I will not be ashamed of it." (2 Corinthians 10:8) Paul does put a qualifier on the extent to which one should boast in 2 Corinthians 10:13: "We, however, will not boast beyond proper limits, but will confine our boasting to the field God has assigned to us."

In the third chapter of Romans, Paul is describing righteousness through faith, apart from observing the law, and is attempting to show how boasting that you have kept the law is futile. The man who is justified is the man who has faith in Jesus. "Where, then, is boasting? It is excluded. On what principle? On that of observing the law? No, but on that of faith." (Romans 3:27) So, again, Paul is teaching that there is no need for boasting about how well you keep the laws that man has laid down. Even when we consider the laws of God, some people like to boast about how they follow God's law to the letter. This is folly, of course, because we know that all have sinned and fallen short of the glory of God, and, as such, are sinful people who are justified through faith rather than "works". If we know that our justification is through our faith in Christ and not our works, why boast about our works! If we must boast, we should boast in the Lord.

Another passage of scripture that is often interpreted to indicate that pride is good is James 1:9-10: "The brother in humble circumstances ought to take pride in his high position. But the one who is rich should take pride in his low position, because he will pass away like a wild flower." Applying this to man's wisdom makes little sense. Why should one be proud of his low position! But, according to God's wisdom, we are taught that everyone, regardless of our "position on earth" is a child of God and has great worth; and, because of this, matters in the Church. Regardless of our capabilities, we should be proud that we have a place in God's church and are in his service, even if it seems to be a "low position". Likewise, the one who is rich should be proud of his humiliation. That is, he (the rich Christian) knows that the THINGS he has, and even his own life, withers like new shoots of grass on a hot day. So he takes pride in knowing that his earthly possessions are nothing. So here James is teaching us that we ought to have pride, BUT that pride should be in our faith in the Lord and in God's wisdom. The pride James is talking about is not based upon our accomplishments, but rather upon our faith.

Occasionally, when a person is reflecting on praise and wondering if there might be a time when a little pride is good, the word confidence pops up. If it is wrong to be proud, maybe we should merely have a lot of confidence in ourselves! Maybe we should use this word to express our pleasure in what we have done or have, etc. Confidence is defined in modern dictionaries as having full trust or belief in something or someone. Self-confidence simply means having full trust in, or reliance on oneself. That gets us into even deeper water, because, again, we fall into that humanistic trap of self-reliance. When we come to believe that we have complete confidence in our own ability, WHO NEEDS GOD! Strangely enough, when we look to God's word for answers as to how we should react to confidence, we find a teaching similar to that regarding pride. Jeremiah tells us: "But blessed is the man who trusts in the Lord, whose confidence is in Him." (Jeremiah 17:7) Jeremiah is not only telling us to put our confidence and trust in the Lord, but he is also telling us we will be blessed if we do! Isaiah also teaches us: "The fruit of righteousness will be peace; the effect of righteousness will be quietness and confidence forever." (Isaiah 32:17) If we do our best to live a righteous life, the effect will be a quiet confidence. This is contrary to the thought behind pride and man's wisdom. The Psalmist David also reflects on where our confidence should be placed. "Though an army besiege me, my heart will not fear; though war break out against me, even then will I be confident." (Psalms 27:3) That is faith! When things really get tough in our lives do we start to worry, get out the tranquilizers, visit a psychiatrist, or do we go to God in prayer and in full confidence know that He is in control. For further confirmation of where we should place our confidence, look at Proverbs 3:25-26: ". . . for the Lord will be your confidence and will keep your foot from being snared." Our foot is snared when we fall into the humanistic trap that teaches us to place all of our confidence in ourselves.

We need to take a close look at what took place when Paul was writing his second letter to the Corinthians. These passages, found primarily in Chapters 11 and 12, are Paul's reaction to a group of false apostles who had gone to Corinth. Apparently, with great cunning, eloquence and self-confidence, either directly, or indirectly, they undermined the work Paul had done there. Throughout these chapters, it appears that Paul is boasting about what he had done. But if we look carefully at the beginning of Chapter 11, we see that Paul starts out by saying: "I hope you will put up with a little of my foolishness . . ." Again, in 11:16-17, Paul says: "I repeat: Let no one take me for a fool. But if you do, then receive me just as you would a fool, so that I may do a little boasting. In this self-confident boasting I am not talking as the Lord would, but as a fool. Since many are boasting in the way the world does, I too will boast." It seems quite clear that Paul detested boasting, apologized for doing it and claimed that it was not the Lord's way, but rather the wisdom of man. However, he would lower himself and boast if it was necessary to get his point across to the Corinthians. So Paul goes on to review his background, telling about his calling, his training as a Pharisee, and all he had suffered physically for the Lord; revealing that he was a Hebrew, an Israelite and a descendant of Abraham, and so on. Right in the middle of all this, probably with a great sigh, he says: "I am out of my mind to talk like this!" In 11:10, Paul says:

"As surely as the truth of Christ is in me, nobody in the regions of Achaia will stop this boasting of mine, if it will cut the ground from under those false apostles." So Paul knew that boasting was wrong. It was clearly distasteful to him, but he would endure it if it were necessary to counter-act the boasting the false apostles were doing in Corinth. If Chapters 10 through 13 are read with these facts in mind, one can better understand where Paul was coming from when he made all the statements which seem to indicate that he condoned pride.

In Chapter 12 Paul relates the story of when he was caught up into paradise where he heard inexpressible things— things about God's plan that man is not permitted to tell. Let's consider the magnitude of that for just a moment. Have you ever been involved in a meeting where the direction of some group, or a plan of action to be taken was decided? Suppose you and several other people had made a decision that was going to affect many others, but only you and a few other people knew what the decision was. Suppose you had to keep this decision confidential for two weeks! In man's world, it would not be unusual for someone in this position to develop an inflated view of his/her importance. Now think of what Paul must have gone through. <u>Paul was lifted into Paradise and saw and heard the plan of God</u>, then came back to earth. Put yourself in his position—an earthly mortal knowing the plan of God! In verse 7 we read: "To keep me from becoming conceited because of these surpassingly great revelations, there was given me a thorn in my flesh . . ." There have been many ideas of what specifically this thorn was, but no one knows for sure. We do know that the thorn was necessary as a con-stant reminder that the revelations Paul had seen and heard were not to be revealed. Rather than being proud because he had seen and heard these things, he was to rely on God's grace—"My grace is sufficient for you, for my power is made perfect in weakness." (Verse 9)

It appears that we are now able to answer the question posed by the title of this chapter—"Isn't a Little Pride OK?" From all the references in the Old and New Testaments, the teaching of the scriptures clearly rings out that pride is a sin. The overwhelming downside of being consumed by pride is that we come to believe that we accomplish things completely on our own—we don't need God. Boasting is not good, but we are told in the scriptures, should we find it necessary to be boastful, we should boast in the Lord and in the work he is doing in the world. If we are proud, we should be proud of our brothers and sisters in Christ and support them in developing their gifts.

We can also glean from the scriptures the advantages of being humble as opposed to being prideful. In Psalm 18:27, David says: "You save the humble but bring low those whose eyes are haughty." And in Psalm 25:9, he says: "He guides the humble in what is right and teaches them his ways." Also, in Proverbs 3:34 we read that God "mocks proud mockers but gives grace to the humble". Also, in one way, man is tested by the way he handles the praise he receives (Proverbs 27:21). Christ also spoke about humility in Matthew 18:4: "Therefore, whoever humbles himself like this child is the greatest in the kingdom of heaven." If we accumulate the virtues listed in the above quoted scriptures, we see that the humble will be saved. They will be shown what is right and what is God's way, and they will be great in God's kingdom. Titus commands us in his brief letter to: ". . .show true humility toward all men". Therefore, we are given numerous examples of why pride is sin; and are not only commanded to be humble, but have listed for us the value of and/or rewards for being humble. Paul sums up the matter in his letter to the Colossians: "Therefore, as God's chosen people, holy and dearly loved, clothe yourself with compassion, kindness, humility, gentleness and patience."

(Colossians 3:12) "As water reflects a face, so a man's heart reflects the man." (Proverbs 27:19) If our hearts are relying and depending on God, we will never become self-centered and prideful, and our inner being will be known by the words that come from our tongue in humility.

FATHER IN HEAVEN, FORGIVE US FOR OUR PRIDEFUL HEARTS. WE ALWAYS SEEM TO WANT TO RATIONALIZE THAT A LITTLE PRIDE IS OK, BUT WE FORGET THAT, WHENEVER WE ACCEPT THAT PRIDE IS OK, WE GIVE IN A LITTLE MORE TO SATAN. WE REALIZE, FATHER, THAT WHEN WE BOAST AND ARE PRIDEFUL, WE ARE REALLY TAKING CREDIT FOR OUR OWN WORK AND ACCOMPLISHMENTS AND ARE ESSENTIALLY LEAVING YOU OUT OF THE PICTURE. WE KNOW IN OUR HEARTS, LORD, THAT YOU ARE OUR SOURCE AND WE SHOULD BE GIVING YOU THE CREDIT FOR WHAT WE ARE AND FOR ALL OUR BLESSINGS. FATHER, WE PRAY FOR HUMBLE HEARTS SO THAT WE MIGHT GLORIFY YOU INSTEAD OF OURSELVES. IN CHRIST'S NAME. AMEN

CHAPTER 4

Pride in Personal Ability

God gave each of us certain abilities. To some He gave exceptional mental capacities, to others He gave exceptional musical talent, to some he gave the ability to help other people, to others he gave the ability to organize an administer, and to still others He gave an extra portion of physical skill that enables them to demonstrate superiority in executing craftsmanship and/or sports skills. These are just a few of the many gifts, or abilities, God has given us in varying amounts. We don't usually find a person who has exceptional ability in many skills, although we sometimes wonder why some individuals seem to be gifted with so many more abilities than others! And, on the other end of the scale, we often see people who seem not to have drawn on any of the gifts available to them.

Ingrained in our secular educational system is the belief that it is necessary, for normal growth and development, to instill in children the value of self worth. We are told that children should develop their self-confidence and discover and develop their unique abilities as they grow. Continually in our schools we teach children to take pride in what they do, or can do. Do you recall someone telling you to take pride in doing a job well, take a little pride in your appearance, or asking don't you want to be proud of the job when it is completed? As parents, we also want our children to do things well and to be proud of their abilities. We praise them and scold them when they do something well or poorly. By the time children finish their schooling, they have become so conditioned to expecting praise that it becomes ingrained in their minds that receiving praise is essential to being psychologically well adjusted. Sometimes we go to the extreme of lowering achievement standards for all, so that a few may experience success and, therefore, praise. Now here is where the problem arises! We are conditioned in our education structure in schools and at home to do well in order to receive praise, and praise becomes so essential to our ego that, when we don't receive praise from others, we praise ourselves! After all, we have been taught that it is good to recognize our abilities; and, if after we have developed certain skills, people are not recognizing and praising us for our achievements, it is only normal to call attention to our abilities in order to gain the recognition we have been conditioned to receive. This need varies tremendously from one individual to another, of course, but the ultimate result of this problem for many people is the development of a prideful attitude. "If people are not going to recognize my talents, I'm going to have to bring them to their attention!"

You may be saying to yourself "right on", Penman, and what's wrong with what you have just explained? After all, that's what we have been taught all of our lives. It can't be all that bad! According to secular psychology, it is not bad. It is, indeed, what we have been taught by man's wisdom all our lives. But, as Christians, we have to look to the Word of God to see whether man's wisdom and God's wisdom are in harmony.

It is very easy to fall into the trap of believing that having pride is good. In Proverbs we read, "The proud and arrogant man—"Mocker" is his name; he behaves with overweening pride." (Proverbs 21:24) Overweening means to be arrogant, excessively proud. Do we have a right to be proud at all? Can we be proud or happy that we have done something well without being conceited about it? Can we be proud without being vain? Pride relates more to our opinion of ourselves, whereas vanity relates to what we would have others think of us. It seems that, if we look at pride as an inner feeling of having done something well, it may be acceptable. One ingredient is still missing, however. If we give ourselves all the credit, it is still sin. We must share the rewards of our accomplishments with our creator, who has given us these abilities. By continually recognizing this source, we cannot become overconfident. Paul, in writing to the Galatians, attempts to differentiate between pride and vanity: "If anyone thinks he is something when he is nothing, he deceives himself. Each one should test his own actions. Then he can take pride in himself, without comparing himself to somebody else, for each one should carry his own load." (Galatians 6:3-4) Paul is actually rebuking vanity and gives us a recipe whereby it may be avoided. We are to compare our achievement not with the work of our neighbors, but with what our best can be, considering what ability the Lord has given us. Some Christians disagree with this viewpoint. They believe that the "best of our ability" belief leaves out the idea of God's anointing. If, however, we believe that God gives varying gifts of all kinds to people, we must recognize that some will have more, or less, of a given gift. We, as intelligent humans, can then develop those gifts or lazily leave them dormant—it's our choice. We must not just sit back and leave it all to God. After all, God put us here to develop, not to merely exist!

More often than not, pride is associated with man's wisdom and/or wickedness. For example, in the book of Job, the Lord said: ". . .look at every proud man and bring him low, look at every proud man and humble him, crush the wicked where thy stand." (Job 40:11-12) David also said: "They (the wicked) close up their callous hearts, and their mouths speak with arrogance." (Psalm 17:10) James teaches: "Likewise the tongue is a small part of the body, but it makes great boasts." (James 3:5) So, from our lips come the boasts that reflect the attitude of our hearts; and those who continually boast, brag and are overconfident about what they have done are indeed wicked according to God's word. The Lord told both Jeremiah and Obadiah in visions that pride is a deceiver. That's why pride is associated with wickedness. Pride deceives us into believing <u>we</u> alone have created and developed our own abilities and, therefore, we have no need to give anyone else credit when, in fact, we should be acknowledging our real source.

Can we examine our own lives and say, like David: "My heart is not proud, O Lord, my eyes are not haughty. . ." (Psalm 131:1). Pride in our personal abilities is a serious matter to God. In Proverbs 18:12, we read: "Before his downfall a man's heart is proud, but humility comes before honor." Pride is the forerunner of man's downfall. As a person becomes more and more prideful of his personal abilities, he begins thinking that he alone is responsible for his successes, and this leads to his downfall in God's eyes. The corporate result of this kind of thinking has led us to embrace secular humanism. But, according to what we read in Proverbs, before we can achieve honor in God's eyes, we must first become humble. It is not God's way, or His wisdom, that says we should take pride in ourselves. Rather, it is man's wisdom—the way we have been brought up. Christ was very clear in this teaching. In fact, He thought it was so important He gave us three examples or teachings to emphasize the importance of being humble. In Matthew 23:12, Luke 14:11, and Luke 18:14, Christ says approximately the same thing: For whoever exalts himself will be humbled, and whoever humbles himself will be exalted. In

Matthew, Christ is showing how the hypocrisy of the proud Pharisees will ultimately lead to their being shut out of the Kingdom. "Everything they do is for men to see." (Matthew 23:5) Christ continues with what are called the seven woes. These seven woes are specific examples of the hypocrisy of the Pharisees, which was a result of their pride, their desire to have men see how great they were. "On the outside you appear to people as righteous, but on the inside you are full of hypocrisy and wickedness." (Matthew 23:28) In the second teaching found in Luke 14:11, Christ is attending a dinner at a prominent Pharisee's home. In the time of Christ, the Jewish custom of having specific places around the table to indicate each person's status was similar to our placing someone at the head of the table today. When Christ saw people taking places of honor on their own at the dinner, he used the parable of the guests at the wedding feast to teach us that, if we deserve recognition, someone else will lead us to our rightful place. If we lead ourselves to a place of honor and our host asks us to move down to a lower place, we will be humiliated and humbled. In the third example, which is found in Luke 18:14, Christ gives us the parable of the Pharisee and the tax collector. The two men went up to the temple to pray. The Pharisee prayed, telling God how closely he was following the law and how he was so much better than the lowly tax collector. The tax collector beat his breast and said, "God, have mercy on me, a sinner." Christ then said that the tax collector, rather than the Pharisee, went home justified before God. These are three specific examples directly from our Lord, saying that He wants us to be humble.

Two great verses from Proverbs also help us know what God thinks of humility. In Proverbs 29:23, we read: "A man's pride brings him low, but a man of lowly spirit gains honor." In Proverbs 27:2, we read: "Let another praise you, and not your own mouth; someone else, and not your own

"For whoever exalts himself will be humbled, and whoever
humbles himself will be exalted."
Matthew 23:12

lips." Notice the similarity of these verses and the teaching of Christ in the three parables shown previously. We are also given a promise in Psalm 25:9: "God guides the humble in what is right and teaches them his way." This promise is so often overlooked. We don't have to take pride in our abilities. Someone else will point out our accomplishments, if appropriate; and God promises us that, if we do remain humble, He will <u>guide us and teach us his ways</u>! If we can remain humble, God will teach us his ways! How much greater it is to be able to discern God's ways and wisdom than merely to have temporary self-gratification. What a promise!

Another proverb that helps us discern how we should handle pride in personal abilities is found in Proverbs 13:10: "Pride only breeds quarrels, but wisdom is found in those who take advice." How true this is! Have you ever observed two individuals discussing their accomplishments, either directly or subtly, and pretty soon they are actually competing or quarreling about who is the greatest. Even the apostles did this. Remember, at the last supper they were questioning Jesus as to who would be the greatest in the Kingdom! STOP—DON'T DO IT! Competing for a high place at God's table is contrary to God's desire. We need to learn to take advice from our brothers and sisters in Christ rather than competing with them for a higher place in God's Kingdom. ". . .and patience is better than pride." (Ecclesiastes 7:8)

A beautiful conclusion to this matter will be seen by examining the words of two teachings in the New Testament. "For everything in the world—the cravings of sinful man, the lust of his eyes and the boasting of what he has and does—comes not from the Father, but from the world. The World and its desires pass away, but the man who does the will of God lives forever." (1 John 2:16) And in Paul's letter to the Philippians he says: "Do nothing out of selfish ambition or vain conceit, (Philippians 2:3) If we could really believe these teachings, memorize them, and live them, we would truly gain God's blessing and come to know more of His wisdom and His ways.

FATHER IN HEAVEN, FORGIVE US FOR EVEN THINKING FOR A MINUTE THAT THINGS WE HAVE OR ABILITIES WE HAVE ARE A RESULT OF OUR OWN EXCLUSIVE ACCOMPLISHMENTS. HELP US TO RECOGNIZE OUR TRUE SOURCE, FATHER, THAT WE OWE OUR GIFTS TO YOU. WE THANK YOU, FATHER, FOR THE ABILITIES YOU HAVE CHOSEN TO GIVE EACH OF US. HELP US TO USE THESE GIFTS TO THE BEST OF OUR ABILITIES AND NOT TO COVET THOSE ABILITIES YOU HAVE CHOSEN TO GIVE TO OTHERS. MAKE US HUMBLE, GOD, SO THAT WE CAN CLAIM YOUR PROMISE THAT YOU WILL TEACH US YOUR WAY. IN CHRITS'S NAME WE PRAY. AMEN

CHAPTER 5

National and Racial Pride

We have all heard the expression "you should be proud you are an American". Most people in a majority of the countries of the world are taught by their society, either indirectly, or directly, that they should be proud to be members of that society. Even within a given country there are various sub units that are knitted together by some common bond, i.e. geography, ethnic origin, language, religion, etc. The tribal system found in many developing countries is one example of this. In America we see the same type of thing between the northern and southern states and eastern and western states. People from foreign countries tend to gravitate toward certain states, and ethnic groups tend to live in certain neighborhoods of cities. Because of their heritage and/or geographical proximity, they develop a pride of association with that "sub-culture". America is made up of people of many different nationalities and races; but, when a national crisis arises, with few exceptions, we unite and display our national pride. This has certainly never been more clearly demonstrated than after the attack on the World Trade Center in New York City. Most Americans believe they live in the greatest nation on the earth. (This is not a boast—rather, it is a fact that few people in the world would deny!)

Sports are another venue for displaying national pride. When a team of any type, be it ice hockey, basketball, volleyball, etc., represents the United States in a foreign country, or a foreign team is playing in America, the pride of the country is at stake and depends on the performance of its team. The epitome of this can be seen every four years in the International Olympics. The opening ceremony includes a parade around the main stadium as teams represent their countries and proudly march behind their country's flag bearers. A country's status in the world is enhanced if it fares well in these contests, and participants have a great deal of pride in representing their respective countries.

My work has provided the opportunity to travel a bit throughout the world. At certain times I am very proud to be an American. We Americans can count on our country to stand behind us. Nearly any place in the world we happen to be, we can go to an American Embassy and receive aid and/or backing from our country. Americans are usually treated quite well by the citizens of other countries. Admittedly, there have been times when I have felt like the proverbial "Ugly American". However, in general, Americans are well respected throughout the world, and we have every right to be proud as a nation—or do we?

International conflicts are constantly occurring throughout the world. Most recently, the Israelis are at odds with the Arab world, we have been in conflicts in Somalia, Bosnia, and Afghanistan. For the first time, the United States mainland has been attacked. In nearly every continent on the face of the earth there is conflict. Whatever happened to the "war to end all wars"? One has only to watch the nightly news and/or read the daily newspapers to see how national pride peaks during a time of national conflict. Wars are the result of many complex issues; however, pride has to be one of the highest considerations when considering the cause of conflict. No country wants to "lose face" in the world's eyes.

"If my people, who are called by my name, will humble themselves and pray and seek my face and turn from their wicked ways, then will I hear from heaven and will forgive their sin and will heal their land."
2 Chronicles 7:14

Closely interwoven with national pride is racial pride. Racial pride can be a problem within a country, but the derivation of the problem is the fact that the varying races ultimately come from different countries. We will deal with this aspect of racial pride in this chapter, and the implications of racial pride as they relate to one human being claiming superiority to another will be dealt with in Chapter 16. Let's take a look at some prideful nations in the history of the world then, possibly, we can have a better perspective of where America stands in the eyes of God today.

From the very beginning of the Jewish family, God made this promise to the people of Abram: "I will make you into a great nation and I will bless you; I will make your name great, and you will be a blessing. I will bless those who bless you, and whoever curses you I will curse; and all peoples on earth will be blessed through you." (Genesis 12:2-3) At the same time God made this covenant with Abram, he wanted the people to place their complete trust and confidence in Him. He could have immediately set up a great empire for the Jews, but did He? No, He first wanted to test them to see if they were capable of trusting in Him. In Deuteronomy 8:2, we read: "Remember how the Lord your God led you all the way in the desert these 40 years, to humble you and to test you in order to know what was in your heart." And in verse 16: "He gave you manna to eat in the desert, something your fathers had never known, to humble and to test you so that in the end it might go well with you." It was not necessary to take 40 years to travel that distance! Today one could leisurely walk the Sinai route Moses took in less than one month! So from the very beginning of the family of Abram, God wanted His nation to have a humble and contrite heart and trust in Him – NOT IN THEIR OWN CORPORATE ABILITIES! Then, in Deuteronomy 26:16, we read: "The Lord your God commands you this day to follow these decrees and laws; carefully observe them with all your heart and with all your soul." And, the writer goes on to say in verse 19, if you do keep my commands: "He has declared that he will set you in praise, fame and honor high above all the nations he has made and that you will be a people holy to the Lord your God, as he promised."

So the Jews became a great nation and multiplied in numbers and land area. But, as with any nation that is very successful in its development, they became proud in what THEY had accomplished. The Lord appeared to Solomon and said: "if my people, who are called by my name, will humble themselves and pray and seek my face and turn from their wicked ways, then will I hear from heaven and will forgive their sin and will heal their land" (2 Chronicles 7:14).

Throughout history He has continually told us, through his messengers, that He wants us as individuals and as nations to be humble and follow His laws. That first lesson in humility in the Sinai desert was not sufficient, He has had to remind his people many times thereafter that they must turn from their wicked ways and then He will heal their land! Amos gives us a glimpse of what God thought of Israel's pride: "Burn leavened bread as a thank offering and brag about your freewill offerings—boast about them, you Israelites, for this is what you love to do," (Amos 4:5). Hosea also records God's relationship with His people when they are so arrogant. "Israel's arrogance testifies against them; the Israelites, even Ephraim, stumble in their sin; Judah also stumbles with them. When they go with their flocks and herds to seek the Lord, they will not find Him; he has withdrawn Himself from them" (Hosea 5:5-6).

God also used Isaiah to record for us the results of national pride and arrogance. Isaiah tells us of the Lord's anger against Israel: "The Lord has sent a message against Jacob; it will fall on Israel. All the people will know it – Ephraim and the inhabitants of Samaria—who say with pride and arrogance of heart, "The bricks have fallen down, but WE will rebuild with dressed stone; the fig trees have been felled, but WE will replace them with cedars" (Isaiah 9:8-10). "But the people have not returned to Him who struck them, nor have they sought the Lord Almighty" (Isaiah 9:13). Ephraim and his clan must have been very proud people for the Lord said He will throw that wreath forcefully to the ground—that wreath, the pride of Ephraim's drunkards will be trampled (paraphrased Isaiah 28:1-3). It seems as though it is "human nature" to want God's blessings WITHOUT following God's laws! Isaiah also prophesied about the fate of Babylon, the jewel of kingdoms, the glory of the Babylonians' pride, will be overthrown by God like Sodom and Gomorrah." (Isaiah 13:19)

Isaiah also tells us about the pride of the Moabites. "We have heard of Moab's pride—her overweening pride and conceit, her pride and her insolence—but her boasts are empty. Therefore the Moabites wail, they wail together for Moab." (Isaiah 16:6-7) And later in 25:11, Isaiah prophesies the fate of Moab: "God will bring down their pride despite the cleverness of their hands."

God is forgiving, and we must be continually grateful for His forgiving nature. God says to Zion: "Though in anger I struck you, in favor I will show you compassion." (Isaiah 60:10) "Although you have been forsaken and hated, with no one traveling through, I will make you the everlasting pride and the joy of all generations. You will drink the milk of nations and be nursed at royal breasts. Then you will know that I, the Lord, am your Savior, your Redeemer, the Mighty One of Jacob." (Isaiah 60:15-16) "For your sake I will send to Babylon and bring down as fugitives all the Babylonians, in the ships in which they took pride. I am the Lord, your Holy One, Israel's Creator, your King." (Isaiah 43:14-15) So, in spite of the prideful nature of the Jews and the many mistakes they made because of their pride and arrogance, God still favors them as a nation SO THAT THEY WILL KNOW

WHO THEIR LORD AND SAVIOR IS!

Then later in the history of the Jews, the cycle repeated itself. God had made Jerusalem a great city and it was not long before the Jews again forgot the source of all their success and became filled with pride and arrogance. "This is what the Lord says: In the same way I will ruin the pride of Judah and the great pride of Jerusalem for following the stubbornness of your own hearts, serving other gods and NOT LISTENING TO ME" (paraphrased Jeremiah 13:9-11). ". . . I will remove from this city those who rejoice in their pride. Never again will you be haughty on my holy hill. But I will leave within you the meek and humble, who trust in the name of the Lord" (Zephaniah 3:11-12).

Other nations and cities were not exempt from God's wrath for their pride and arrogance. "Now this was the sin of your sister Sodom: She and her daughters were arrogant, overfed and unconcerned; they did not help the poor and needy. They were haughty and did detestable things before me. Therefore I did away with them as you have seen." (Ezekiel 16:49-50) Ezekiel also Prophesied about the fate of the people of Tyre because of their pride: "In the pride of your heart you say, "I am a god;" . . ."They will bring you down to the pit, and you will die a violent death in the heart of the seas. Will you then say, "I am a god, . . . ". (Ezekiel 28:2; 8-9) Egypt's pride was also shattered and compared to the cedar tree: "Therefore this is what the sovereign Lord says, "Because it towered on high, lifting its top above the thick foliage, and because it was proud of its height, I handed it over to the ruler of the nations, for him to deal with accordingly to its wickedness. I cast it aside, and the most ruthless of foreign nations cut it down and left it." (Ezekiel 31:10) They will shatter the pride of Egypt, and all her hordes will be overthrown." (Ezekiel 32:12) Edom was so proud that they actually boasted that they did not need God! "You boasted against me and spoke against me without restraint, and I heard it . . . I WILL MAKE YOU DESO-LATE." (Ezekiel 35:13-14)

There are numerous additional examples throughout history from the Biblical and secular records that illustrate what happens to nations who become so arrogant and prideful that they reject God. The root of national pride is the same as the root of personal pride. That is, a nation becomes so elated with its accomplishments that it soon believes it has reached its heights on its own. If that be the case, who needs God! What have we learned from history? One reason historians give for studying history is that we might learn from past mistakes and prevent them from occurring in the future. It looks as though we missed again! How does America stand in God's sight today? Are we a proud nation? Are we following God's law? Do we reject God and say that we are so successful that we don't need God anymore? Or are we a God-fearing nation following His commandments?

When our great country was founded, it was indeed blessed by God. It is impossible to conceive how America could possibly have become the greatest country to have ever existed in history in only a few hundred years if it had not been by the grace of God. Most of the founding fathers of our country were Bible believing men who established "one nation under God". The last sentence of the Declaration of Independence states: "And for the support of this Declaration, with a firm Reliance on the Protection of Divine Providence, we mutually pledge to each other our Lives, our Fortunes, and our sacred Honor." The first amendment of the Constitution of the United States, ratified December 17, 1791, reads: "Congress shall make no law respecting an establishment of religion, or prohibiting the free exercise thereof; . . ." During the intervening 211 years our society has changed considerably. I doubt very much that the founding fathers had in mind, when they developed the Constitution and its Amendments, the justification of homosexuality, legalized abortion, legalized suicide and euthanasia, justification of children suing school boards for removing pornographic materials from school libraries, making celebration of Christmas in schools illegal, or preventing children from having the OPTION of having a time of prayer in schools! We have strayed so far from the dependence on God our nation's founders had, that many "modern day prophets" are suggesting it may be too late for America. We may have gone too far.

Secular humanism, with its associated atheism and/or agnosticism, has become so established as the National Religion in our courts and our national educational system that it may indeed be too late for America. Americans, in general, have been duped into believing that we are so great, so invincible, and so intellectual that we do not need to believe in a God. Consequently, the common belief is our country is the greatest because of what WE have done. Look at this quotation from the Humanist Manifesto II. "We find insufficient evidence for belief in the existence of a supernatural; it is either meaningless or irrelevant to the question of the survival and fulfillment of the human race. As nontheists, we begin with humans not God, nature not deity." With this doctrine prevalent in the legal and educational leadership of our country, we are surely repeating history! We are led to believe by the humanists that God is a creation of man and that man can solve all the problems of the world; if, of course, given enough time! As we continue to slide down this slippery slope, will God desert us! Why do we think that we will be any different than other great countries throughout history? It is a fact of history. All nations who become arrogant and filled with pride FALL! We have seen it time and time again; yet, we think we are different for some reason. Great nations of the past have fallen because God has abandoned them after they have denied their dependence on Him. Earlier in this chapter, we saw repeatedly that, time after time, nations fell for two basic reasons. They began living in opposition to God's law, and they became so proud of their accomplishments that they no longer believed they needed to be dependent on God. God has dealt severely with nations in the past, and He will do the same with America unless we change our direction drastically and quickly.

DEAR FATHER IN HEAVEN, FORGIVE US OUR SINS AS A NATION. WE KNOW WE HAVE STRAYED FROM THE IDEALS ESTABLISHED BY OUR FOREFATHERS, WHICH RECOGNIZED AND GLORIFIED YOU. FATHER, WE KNOW, IF WE DO NOT CHANGE THE DIRECTION OUR NATION IS TAKING, WE DO NOT DESERVE THE BLESSINGS YOU HAVE GIVEN US, AND THEY WILL BE TAKEN AWAY FROM US. HELP US INDIVIDUALLY, TO DO WHATEVER WE CAN TO HELP RESTORE OUR COUNTRY ONCE AGAIN TO ITS RELIANCE UPON YOU FOR ALL ITS NEEDS AND TO MAKE OUR CITIZENS RECOGNIZE THAT YOUR LAWS WERE GIVEN FOR OUR BENEFIT. IN CHRIST'S NAME. AMEN.

CHAPTER 6

Pride of Association

A very common trait that we humans have is to take pride in an association of some sort. It is common to hear a person boasting about the fact that they know someone famous. Hey! Did you know that I talked to the Governor at a meeting one time? Do you know that I went to school with so and so? I once had Tiger Woods in a class I taught! I had a great time the other day having lunch with the mayor of our city! I saw a great motion picture star at the airport, and he spoke to me! I knew her before she became famous! Ad infinitum. In addition to boasting about individuals with whom we have associated, we tend to boast about our association with a group. This phenomenon is easily seen in relation to sports. Almost everyone has experienced the "super fans" that advertise their team with clothing, wave flags and scream at the top of their lungs at games! This is a common occurrence in the sports world.

For some reason, people like to be associated with someone or something. We seem to have a need to feel important by letting people know that we have an association with someone who is recognized publicly. Why, as Christians, do we need this pride of association with other individuals or groups when we have the ultimate in friendship in our relationship with other believers, and in Jesus Christ. Let's first take a look at what the Word says about boasting about our association with others, then we will examine in depth the ultimate relationship—one with Jesus Christ.

When we examine Paul's teaching on relationships, we find that he emphasized we should be proud of our association with other believers. In spite of the fact that the early church was enduring many hardships and persecutions, Paul found great joy and pride in his associations with other believers. In his second letter to the Corinthians he states: "I have great confidence in you; I take great pride in you. I am greatly encouraged; in all our troubles my joy knows no bound" (2 Corinthians 7:4). He felt this great pride because of the steadfast faith and concern the brethren had for one another.

On another occasion Paul had reason to reprimand the believers for being too prideful regarding their associations. Christians of that day were clustering around a particular "spiritual leader" and were tending to be followers of a specific persons i.e. Paul, Apollos, and Cephas, rather than followers of Christ. "Now, brothers, I have applied these things to myself and Apollos for your benefit, so that you may learn from us the meaning of the saying, "Do not go beyond what is written." Then you will not take pride in one man over against another" (1 Corinthians 4:6). Doesn't this sound a bit familiar to our day? It seems very easy for Christians today to cluster around a particular evangelist, preacher, and/or teacher and soak up everything that person has to say; and, thereby, become followers, in varying degrees, of the MAN! Certainly, some teachers and preachers have more charisma than others, and may be better teachers and preachers than others, and because of this it is very easy to become more influenced by the method than by the message. As Paul points out, we have to be constantly on guard against this problem. We must not become so prideful that we follow a particular man. We can quickly become "church hoppers" trying to find the best teachers, preachers, comfortable pews, etc., when we should really be seeking a way to serve and be fed where we are.

Paul expresses a very profound truth related to pride of association in his first letter to the Corinthians. "We are not trying to commend ourselves to you again, but are giving you an opportunity to take pride in us, so that you can answer those who take pride in what is seen rather than what is in the heart" (2 Corinthians 5:12). Our "human nature" makes it so much easier to take pride in a brother or sister who has done something well, has achieved something great, or has obtained something that has great value. We often take great pride in knowing the Christian athlete or the Christian astronaut, for example, yet have little pride in our association with a quiet humble servant of God who has a great heart, but has no fame in man's eyes! This is precisely what Paul was talking about. We should take pride in our brothers and sisters in Christ who keep the steadfast faith and are humble, in spite of the fact that, according to worldly standards, they have done nothing or achieved nothing worthy of pride. To be sure, there are many Christians in the public eye who have genuine hearts for Christ, but as Christians we should be just as proud of all our brothers regardless of their "station in life". To befriend a "nobody" is not nearly as gratifying as befriending someone who is well known—yet, God knows our hearts, and we know from His Word that ". . . whatever you did for one of the least of these brothers of mine, you did for me." (Matthew 25:40)

Later in Paul's letter he presents another important lesson on pride of association when he instructs the church to show its love for one another. "Therefore show these men the proof of your love and the reason for our pride in you, so that the churches can see it." (2 Corinthians 8:24) We should give praise to the Lord when we see Christians expressing

**"Be completely humble and gentle; be patient,
bearing with one another in love."
Ephesians 4:2**

love to others, for this is essential to the Christian walk. Can you imagine how Satan delights every time he hears Christians put each other down in public! Non-Christians are quick to show how Christians are constantly bickering among themselves. They delight in pointing out the hypocrisy among Christians. On the other side, we are really joyful when we see Christians of different denominations and/or beliefs hugging each other and sharing their common faith in Jesus Christ. We need to do this more. We need to accentuate Christian love and eliminate emphasizing the negative differences and show non-believers that we are proud to be in the "family of God"! Peter tells us: ". . . have sincere love for your brothers, love one another deeply, from the heart." (1 Peter 1:22) That doesn't mean just those Christians in your local church. Peter means all the brothers and sisters in Christ scattered throughout the world!

We are commissioned as believers to be humble; not only regarding our own abilities, but also in our relation-ships. "Be completely humble and gentle; be patient, bear-ing with one another in love." (Ephesians 4:2) The apostle Peter also tells us how we ought to relate to one another: "Finally, all of you, live in harmony with one another; be sympathetic, love as brothers, be compassionate and hum-ble." (1 Peter 3:8) And later in Chapter 5, verse 6, Peter says: "Humble yourselves, therefore, under God's mighty hand, that he may lift you up in due time."

When considering pride of association, we must also examine the concept of false humility. We have already seen in previous chapters that often a person may be boasting in their humility—"I have more humility than anyone else in the group". Paul also gives us a few words on this sin. "Do not let anyone who delights in false humility and the wor-ship of angels disqualify you for the prize." (Colossians 2:18) That's a pretty strong admonishment! Paul is saying that if we fake it, that is, if we act as though we are humble when, in fact, we are boasting, we may not win the prize!

It appears that God wants us to be genuinely humble in our relations with others. We should not boast about our association with others merely for our own gratification, or to look good in the eyes of others; but, rather, should take pride in seeing fellow Christians living God's love and cherish associations in the depths of our hearts.

Now let's examine our association with our "friend" Jesus Christ. I'll bet nearly every American has, at some time, sung these words: "What a friend we have in Jesus . . .Can we find a friend so faithful who will all our sorrows share . . ." According to OPERATION WORLD, 21st CENTURY EDITION, 84.53 per cent of the American population is Christian. I'm sure you are familiar with the term "name dropper"—a person who throws out the name of a famous acquaintance in order to impress someone. It's my belief that many of the millions of people in the world who profess to "know" Jesus Christ are "name droppers"! Often it is the "in thing" to claim to be a Christian and say you know Jesus Christ. When we claim to be a "friend" of Jesus are we merely name dropping in order to make ourselves feel good and/or gain acceptance by our peers, or do we really have a personal relationship with Christ that goes far beyond earthly friendship?

In order to further examine pride of personal relationships, let's take a close look at what is involved in friendship. Let's follow an imaginary dialogue and say that a number of years ago I had a student in class who is very prominent in the sports world. Let's say his name is Tiger Woods (by the way, I did not have Tiger Woods in class). The conversation might go something like the following. WOW! My friend Tiger is a great guy! I could tell you a lot of things about my ol' friend Tiger. Now, you might really be impressed by the fact that I knew Tiger Woods, but what possible motive could I have for giving you this information except to brag about an association. Let's look at some of the essentials of this feigned "friendship". What does the name Tiger mean? Well, uh, I don't know. I know it's on a lot of stuff. Where was he born? Well, I'm not sure. Do you know much about his life? Not really! He did well in my class, but I really didn't get to know him that well. Do you know what he believes, or stands for? Well, I have seen him on television several times, and he has said some very good things! Do you know his real character? No, I guess not! Do you know what his future is? No! Does your friend Tiger know you? Well, er, uh, I doubt it. But what a friend I have in Tiger Woods!!!

Now let's take a look at our "friendship" with Jesus Christ and see if we really know Him, or are we merely name dropping! The name Jesus is not a unique name now, nor was it during biblical times. But Jesus the Christ means the one with the common name Jesus who is the Messiah, the coming one, the Son of God! So His name is very unique, because it identifies a person in history who was both human and divine. What do we know about His birth? We know Jesus was born of a virgin (Matthew 1:23). We know He was born of the Holy Spirit (Matthew 1:20). We do not know the exact time He was born; however, His birth probably took place sometime during the summer—"And there were shepherds living out in the fields nearby, keeping watch over their flocks at night." (Luke 2:8) What did he look like? We don't really know. We have had many artists paint portraits of what they think Christ might have looked like, however; few, if any, match the bits of information we have in the scriptures! Jesus was the oldest son of a carpenter (today this type of job would be called a contractor). You don't generally find fair skinned, effeminate looking men around the construction industry! There are several convincing bits of scripture that allow us to believe that Jesus did not have long hair. For example, why would the Lord inspire

Paul to write to the Corinthians, "Does not the very nature of things teach you that if a man has long hair, it is a disgrace to him" (1 Corinthians 11:14) if Christ himself had had long hair. Some people believe Christ had long hair because he was from Nazareth. Jesus did grow up in Nazareth, but He was not a Nazarite. Nazarites had long hair, did not drink wine, did not touch the dead, etc. So we must not rely on artists to give us an image of what Christ may have looked like, but rather, search the Word for that information. "He had no beauty or majesty to attract us to him, nothing in his appearance that we should desire him" (Isaiah 53:2). It is probably a good thing the camera had not been developed when Christ was on earth, or people would still be worshipping pictures of the man! In fact, Christ looked so ordinary that several times he got lost in the crowds (John 8:59, 10:39). It is hard to imagine a beautiful man with a long white robe, with long golden locks of hair, with a halo over his head, and a luminescence about his body (things artists use to create an image of Christ) being able to get lost in a crowd! One could pick out a person like this in a coliseum holding 100,000 people! Jesus was the eldest son in a rather large family. He had four brothers-James, Joseph, Simon, Judas, and at least two sisters—a total of at least 9 members in the family of Mary and Joseph (Matthew 13:55-56). Then, as today, the eldest son often helped run the family business, so it is very possible that Jesus was helping his father in his contracting business until the beginning of His public ministry (about age 30!). Jesus did pay taxes! "After Jesus and his disciples arrived in Capernaum, the collectors of the two drachma tax came to Peter and asked, "Doesn't your teacher pay the temple tax?" "Yes he does," he replied" (Matthew 17:24-25). Jesus associated with all levels of society. He healed lepers, poor people, and the wealthy. He associated socially with Pharisees, tax collectors, publicans, and many others. Our friend Jesus ministered wherever there was a need. One of the goals on earth of our "friend" is specifically stated in Luke 4:43: "I must preach the good news of the kingdom of God to the other towns also, because that is why I was sent." So Christ might be called the first missionary. We also know our "friend" was convicted in a mock trial and sentenced to death. We know He was killed for that which He was innocent of and was buried behind a sealed tomb that was guarded by a group of Roman soldiers. We know that He arose from the dead after three days in that guarded tomb. We also know that if Christ has not been raised, all preaching is useless and so is our faith! How can we possibly call Jesus our friend if we do not believe these basic truths! Surely, most of us know far more about Jesus than we would about Tiger Woods after a slight acquaintance, but whom would we be most anxious to claim as our friend?

These are just some of the highlights of Christ's life that are used to illustrate this point. If you are going to boast about your friendship with Christ, then you ought to know who He was, who He claimed to be, and who He is today!

Christ is indeed MUCH more than a mere friend. Christ is the door to eternal salvation and we all have to make a decision to knock on that door and ask Christ to let us in His Kingdom. The Lord himself talks to us plainly about boasting. "This is what the lord says: "Let not the wise man boast of his wisdom or the strong man boast of his strength or the rich man boast of his riches, but let him who boasts boast about this: THAT HE UNDERSTANDS AND KNOWS ME, THAT I AM THE LORD, WHO EXERCISES KINDNESS, JUUSTICE AND RIGHTEOUSNESS ON EARTH, FOR IN THESE I DELIGHT" declares the Lord." (Jeremiah 9:24-24) Yes, what a friend we have in Jesus, and, we are also His friends! "You are my friends if you do what I command." (John 15:14) "Love each other as I have loved you. Greater love has no one than this, that one lay down his life for his friends." (John 15: 12-13) Are we willing to lay down our lives for that ultimate friend?

FATHER, WHAT A PRIVILEGE IT IS TO KNOW YOU; NOT ONLY AS A FRIEND, BUT ALSO AS LORD AND AS SAVIOR. FATHER, FORGIVE US FOR MIS-PLACED EMPHASIS ON OUR FRIENDSHIPS HERE ON EARTH. WE TAKE GREAT PRIDE IN BOASTING ABOUT OUR ASSOCIATIONS WITH PROMINENT PEOPLE OR PROMINENT GROUPS JUST TO BUILD UP OUR EGOS. FATHER, HELP US TO PLACE PRIDE WHERE IT BELONGS—IN OUR BROTHERS AND SIS-TERS WHO ARE LIVING YOUR WILL AND IN OUR RELATIONSHIP WITH YOU, THE MOST IMPORTANT RELATIONSHIP WE CAN EVER HAVE. REMOVE THIS PRIDE OF ASSOCIATION FROM OUR HEARTS NOW, LORD. IN JESUS' NAME WE PRAY. AMEN

CHAPTER 7

Pride in Material Possessions

There have been many books and articles written on the topic of how much a Christian should possess in the way of material goods. There are those who believe that we should share everything we have with the needy; and, as a result, never have much "stored up" in the way of material goods. There are others who believe that it is OK to be wealthy if we are generous with our wealth and that having wealth places them in a better position to give more to the Lord's work. Hannah, mother of the prophet and judge of Israel, Samuel, had this to say about our financial status: "The Lord sends poverty and wealth; he humbles and he exalts." (1 Samuel 2:7) Often we hear it said that we are lucky to live in America where "everyone is wealthy". You can hear that statement over and over, but it doesn't sink in until you have seen, with your own eyes, how the rest of the world's people live. People in the slums of America seem wealthy when compared to others in certain parts of the world! Therefore, the term wealthy is a relative statement and needs to be compared to something. We will not discuss here why God chooses to allow some people to have more material things than others or why some always seem to remain in poverty. Rather, we are concerned here with how people handle the "wealth" they have.

The problem for Christians is not how much we have in the way of material possessions, but what is the source of our wealth, what do we do with it, are we humble or proud because of what the Lord has given us. We see numerous examples in God's Word of how pride of material possessions has been a stumbling block to God's people throughout history. Ezekiel gave a prophecy against the Mountains of Israel and enumerated the sins of the people. Included in this list was the sin of pride in material possessions: "They were proud of their beautiful jewelry and used it to make their detestable idols and vile images. Therefore, I will turn these into an unclean thing for them. I will hand it all over as plunder to foreigners and as loot to the wicked of the earth, and they will defile it." (Ezekiel 7:20-21) Of course, that was in the "old days", we don't worship and covet beautiful jewelry today! Do we?

In the book of Esther we are given another example of pride of possessions. Haman, the son of Hammedatha, the Agagite, received an honored position with King Xerxes. Haman actually wanted to destroy all the Jews; but one particular Jew named Mordecai really bothered him, because he continually refused to give him any respect. Calling together his friends and his wife, "Haman boasted to them about his vast wealth, his many sons, and all the ways the king had honored him and how he had elevated him above the other nobles and officials." (Esther 5:11) Haman's boasting about his possessions and status was temporary, because he was shortly hanged on the very gallows he had built for the purpose of hanging Mordecai. Have you ever boasted about a material possession? "Look at my new car! It cost a bundle, but look at all the features it has!" "We have to have three cars in our family for everyone to be able to get around! "You just have to see our new furniture!" "Look at my new diamond ring!" Having these things may not be a sin; however, boasting to others about them is! One could say the possessions have become idols. "All who worship images are put to shame, those who boast in idols . . .". (Psalm 97:7) Many people today believe that your God is that in which you place most of your money and time. In that sense, many of us are guilty of worshipping idols, since we spend so much of our time and money in acquiring material possessions, whose need is often questionable, and then boasting to others about having them.

One of the richest men to have ever lived on earth was King Solomon. He received millions of dollars yearly from Arabian kings, merchants and traders. All his shields were made of gold. His throne was made of ivory and gold. All of his housewares were made of gold. Silver was considered of minor value even in those days! He had fleets of trading ships, fourteen hundred chariots and twelve thousand horses. His home took 13 years to build. "King Solomon was greater in riches and wisdom than all the other kings of the earth." (1 Kings 10:23) In his later days Solomon wrote the book of Ecclesiastes and in 5:10 says: "Whoever loves money never has money enough; whoever loves wealth is never satisfied with his income." He should know, because he spent a lifetime building a vast treasury. Solomon must have been very proud of all the material things he possessed; yet, in his later days, he said that patience is better than pride. He said that all this accumulation of material things is a chasing after the wind—it is meaningless. The conclusion this wealthy and wise man, who had everything, came to was that all this earthly stuff is meaningless! "The essence of life is fearing God and keeping His commandments, for this is the whole duty of man." (Ecclesiastes 12:13) Solomon was indeed wise. Even though he did have problems with sin, in his older days he realized that the important thing in life was not acquiring material things, rather it was being patient, fearing God, and keeping His commands.

That is precisely our duty as Christians today. It is not uncommon to hear of very wealthy people taking their own lives. They find no satisfaction in the accumulation of material things and see life as meaningless. If only they would listen to what Solomon had to say!

Three verses from Proverbs 22 also speak to how we should handle material wealth. "A good name is more desirable than great riches; to be esteemed is better than silver or gold." "Rich and poor have this in common: The Lord is the Maker of them all." "Humility and the fear of the Lord bring wealth and honor and life." (Proverbs 22:1, 2 and 4) The first proverb clearly states that the essence of life is not what we have, but rather what we are. Having a "good name" means that a person possesses good character; i.e. he is honest, trustworthy, obedient to God, etc.; and because of these traits, he is held in high esteem. If material prosperity should happen to accompany these traits, then that is merely an added gift the Lord has given us to test our ability to handle it! Many people do not look at material prosperity in that way. We usually tend to think that the more material goods one has, the happier he is. NOT TRUE! There are literally millions of people throughout the world who have nothing in the way of material goods, yet are very happy people! Having a lot of material possessions can be a very frustrating experience to the Christian and becomes a very real testing as to how he is able to handle prosperity and, at the same time, retain "his good name".

The second proverb mentioned above reminds us that the sovereign God made us all—rich and poor alike. Why God chooses to give some of us more than others we will never know, but it is certain that God wants us to know that developing character and pleasing Him are more important than having material things. Then in the third proverb noted above we see that humility and the fear of the Lord bring wealth and honor and life. If we develop a humble attitude,

"For everything in the world—the cravings of sinful man,
the lust of his eyes and the boasting of what he has and
does—comes not from the Father but the world."
1 John 2:16

that is, acquire a modest sense of our own abilities and recognize that what we are and have is indeed a gift from God, we will have true wealth, honor and life. How contrary this is to man's way. We have an inherent value in American society that implies that the more material things we have, the more value we have as a person. As a result, we have a desire to share with society how well we are doing if we are prosperous. This is where pride enters; but, according to the teachings of Proverbs, we Christians learn that true wealth, honor and a happy life come from a humble spirit.

In Psalm 49 we have a beautiful discourse on the relationship of boasting about great riches and the ultimate fate of all people. "Why should I fear when evil days come, when wicked deceivers surround me—those who trust in their wealth and boast of their great riches?" (Psalm 49:5-6) "Do not be overawed when a man grows rich, when the splendor of his house increases; for he will take nothing with him when he dies, his splendor will not descend with him. Though while he lived he counted himself blessed—and men praise you when you prosper—he will join the generation of his fathers, who will never see the light of life. A man who has riches without understanding is like the beasts that perish." (Psalm 49:16-20) The last phrase is the key! A man who has riches without realizing what the source of those riches is and boasts about HIS ability to accumulate those riches, simply does not acknowledge his creator and winds up perishing like the beast. But, for the rich and poor alike, we have a promise that if we remain humble and give God credit for all our riches, whatever they are, then: "God will redeem my soul from the grave; he will surely take me to himself." (Psalm 49:15) Wow! What a promise!

The prophet Hosea, writing about the decaying lifestyle of the people in the Northern Kingdom around 730 B.C., tells us that the people became so wealthy and so prideful that they believed they didn't need God—they could make their own gods! In fact, they became so haughty that they didn't even recognize right from wrong. Ephraim boasts, "I am very rich; I have become wealthy. With all my wealth they will not find in me any iniquity or sin." (Hosea 12:8) This, of course, was very distasteful to God, and the rest of the book of Hosea expresses the Lord's anger against Israel. Even though this occurred about 2700 years ago, is it really any different in our society today? We have become so enamored with our materialistic society that we are essentially saying today that we don't need God. With secular humanism rampant in our educational and legal system, we, as a nation, have become so prideful that "man" (secular humanism would have us believe) has created God! When this happens we, as a nation, lose all perspective as to what is right and what is wrong. We are not even capable of recognizing sin as sin! It is no wonder, then, that many people believe there is nothing wrong with taking the life of an unborn child, there is nothing wrong with spewing vulgarity and profanity, there is nothing wrong with polluting our minds with drugs, ad infinitum! Our gods today have become intellectualism and materialism! It is easy to look back 2700 years and condemn the Jews for their prideful conduct and heathenism and smugly read of God's condemnation of that conduct. Yet, today, our conduct is no different. Can we really expect a different reaction by God to us as a nation?

In the first epistle, John summarizes God's viewpoint of this subject by telling us "straight out" His feelings on man's boasting about his material possessions: "For everything in the word—the cravings of sinful man, the lust of his eyes and the boasting of what he has done—comes not from the Father but from the world. The world and its desires pass away, but the man who does the will of God lives forever." (1 John 2:16-17) In Jeremiah 9 the Lord said: "Let not the rich man boast of his riches. . .but let him who boasts boast about this: that he understands and knows me, that I am the Lord, who exercises kindness, justice, and righteousness on earth, for in these I delight."

Indeed, we have a wealth of material things which make our lives more comfortable, but we must not let them become our gods. We need to constantly remind ourselves of the source of our lives and all material things and constantly give praise to God for those things He has given us.

FATHER IN HEAVEN, FORGIVE US AS INDIVIDU-ALS AND AS A NATION FOR BEING SO HAUGHTY AND PRIDEFUL THAT WE GET DISTRACTED BY WORLDLY OCCURRENCES AND TURN FROM YOUR WAYS. HELP US TO REMEMBER THAT IT IS YOUR DESIRE THAT WE WORSHIP YOU AS OUR TRUE GOD AND THAT THESE LITTLE THINGS WE ACQUIRE IN LIFE ARE TRANSITORY. HELP US TO BE TRULY HUMBLE AND THANKFUL FOR THE THINGS WE HAVE AND TO ACKNOWLEDGE THAT ALL THINGS COME FROM YOU, AND AS GOOD STEW-ARDS, WE ARE TO USE THEM TO YOUR BENEFIT. IN YOUR SON'S NAME WE PRAY. AMEN

CHAPTER 8

Pride in Appearance

Here we have a topic that is very dear to everyone. In our secular upbringing we are constantly told to have pride in our appearance, but very seldom do we look to the scriptures to really find out what God wants us to be like in our appearance or how we should view our appearance. Our appearance really consists of several components. It involves the clothing we wear, our speech, physical fitness level, grooming, and personal hygiene (cleanliness, use of deodorants, makeup, etc.). There is a rather popular song that essentially says: It's hard to be humble when you are so great in every way!" How true this is! If one is truly beautiful and has a well proportioned body it is very difficult to be humble; because in all walks of society good looks and "sexual appeal" have been exploited to encourage pride in appearance, and this sell products! I suppose we could establish a "law" related to pride of appearance. The more perfect a person is, that is, the greater the number of personal attributes one has, the more difficult it is to be truly humble. There is an inverse relation between the two traits. One could also make a parallel law that states that the degree of pride in appearance is proportional to the amount of time a person spends in front of a mirror, but we won't do that because we don't want to get too personal!!

There are numerous examples in the Word describing people who are gifted with a beautiful appearance. Occasionally we are given details of this beauty and other times we are not. Abram's wife Sarai was, according to Abram, a very beautiful woman. When they went to Egypt Abram was afraid that because of her beauty the Egyptians would kill him and take her if they knew she was his wife. "When Abram came to Egypt, the Egyptians saw that she was a very beautiful woman. And when Pharaoh's officials saw her, they praised her to Pharaoh, and she was taken into his palace" (Genesis 12:14-15). So apparently it was not only Abram's biased opinion that Sarai was beautiful. Since the Egyptian officials also praised her for her beauty, she must have been a truly beautiful woman.

In 2 Samuel we read of the handsome Absalom: "In all Israel there was not a man so highly praised for his handsome appearance as Absalom. From the top of his head to the sole of his foot there was no blemish in him." (2 Samuel 14:25) "Three sons and a daughter were born to Absalom. His daughter's name was Tamar, and she became a beautiful woman" (2 Samuel 14:27). King David had a ruddy complexion, fine appearance and handsome features, according to 1 Samuel 16:12. We are not given much detail in the scriptures about how these people handled their potential pride problem due to their beautiful appearance. We can only imagine that they would have the same struggle as a person who is struggling with pride in appearance today.

Isaiah probably gives us the most harshly worded admonishment by the Lord on the misuse of beauty. The Lord says, "The women of Zion; the Lord will make their scalps bald. In that day the Lord will snatch away their finery; the bangles and headbands and crescent necklaces, the earrings and bracelets and veils, the headdresses and ankle chains and sashes, the perfume bottles and charms, the signet rings and nose rings, the fine robes and the capes and cloaks, the purses and mirrors, and the linen garments and tiaras and shawls. Instead of fragrance there will be a stench; instead of a sash, a rope; instead of well-dressed hair, baldness; instead of fine clothing, sackcloth; instead of beauty, branding" (Isaiah 3:16-24). These women were haughty or proud because of their appearance. Do you know anybody today who is obviously proud because of their good looks?

The importance of beauty, of course, varies in different societies. I am reminded of an incident that occurred when I was a teenager. I was working for a manufacturing company in the Los Angeles area, and it was customary for the workers to eat their lunch in front of the plant so that they might also enjoy "standing on the corner watching all the girls go by". At the same time, of course, aesthetical value judgments would be made. One middle aged man from a foreign country never would make a comment as the others did until one day a short, overweight woman passed by. According to him, she should have been "Miss universe"; and he was very serious about it. According to his standards she was indeed a very beautiful woman! Indeed, the perception of beauty varies from place to place, person to person.

Apparently it is not the beauty itself that creates the pride problem; after all, that is also a gift from our creator. Rather, the potential problem relates to how well the individual appreciates and uses that gift. The women of Zion were possessed with the desire to "look beautiful". They wore excessive jewelry and makeup, were constantly looking in the mirror, maintained fancy hair styles, wore fancy clothes and used exotic perfumes. The thing that was displeasing to the Lord was that their beauty was a source of conceit! It would be very easy to show a parallel between the women of Zion and the "modern woman" of today. Christians must continually ask: What is the purpose of this pride in appearance? Why am I trying to look so fancy?

"Charm is deceptive, and beauty is fleeting; but a woman
who fears the Lord is to be praised."
Proverbs 31:30

"Why dress yourself in scarlet and put on jewels of gold? Why shade your eyes with paint? You adorn yourself in vain . . . " (Jeremiah 4:30). The answer is simply, this is what society has led us to believe is desirable!

Here we have another prime example of how man's way is different from God's way. In Proverbs 31:30 we read: "Charm is deceptive, and beauty is fleeting; but a woman who fears the Lord is to be praised." So here we are instructed to praise the woman who stands in awe of, or fears the Lord. For this is the most important quality a person can have. The character we are developing on earth is eternal, whereas the physical beauty we possess is fleeting. "A wife of noble character who can find? She is worth far more than rubies. Her husband has full confidence in her and lacks nothing of value" (Proverbs 31:10-11). In the process of Samuel's anointing of David to be king, Samuel did not know whom God had chosen. On Samuel's arrival in Bethlehem, he saw Eliab and thought he was the one God had chosen because of his majestic appearance. "But the Lord said to Samuel, "Do not consider his appearance or his height, for I have rejected him. The Lord does not look at the things man looks at. Man looks at the outward appearance, but the Lord hooks at the heart" (1 Samuel 16:7) Again, the problem is not with beauty itself. Paul explains the essence of the problem in Romans 8:5: "Those who live according to the sinful nature have their minds set on what that nature desires; but those who live in accordance with the Spirit, have their minds set on what the Spirit desires." In the Goodspeed Version of the Bible, Romans 8:5 reads: "People who are controlled by the physical think of what is physical." If we over-emphasize the physical, we will most likely be neglecting the spiritual. Our Lord apparently did not come to us on earth as a big handsome man: "He had no beauty or majesty to attract us to him, nothing in his appearance that we should desire him . . ." (Isaiah 53:2) He came so that in believing in Him we might have eternal life-not so that we could admire a temporal, handsome human!

In addition to our "natural physical attributes", that is those genetic qualities we inherit, our appearance is also influenced by what we do in the way of maintenance of our physical bodies. We don't have anything to say about our inherited genes, but we have a great deal to say about how we take care of this God-given body-whatever form it may be. The classic scripture used to illustrate this point is found in Paul's first letter to the Corinthians: "Don't you know that you yourselves are God's temple and that God's Spirit lives in you? If anyone destroys God's temple, God will destroy him; for God's temple is sacred, and you are that temple." (1 Corinthians 3:16-17) So we have a very strong responsibility to maintain our bodies at a high level. This, too, can be carried to an extreme. An individual who spends too much time primping can become very narcissistic. That is, he can become "in love" with his /her own appearance, through an erotic gratification derived from admiration of his/her own physical or mental attributes. Narcissus, according to Greek legend, was a beautiful young man who one day noticed his reflection in a calm pool of water, and saw how beautiful he was. Thereafter he "fell in Love" with his own appearance. Even though Narcissus was a legendary figure, the meaning of the term narcissism certainly exemplifies pride in one's own appearance. So even though we are responsible to "look after" our appearance we should not become so infatuated with our physical appearance that we over-emphasize the physical when, in fact, our spiritual relationship with the Lord should be of primary importance.

The Word even gives advice for those who enjoy and emphasize physical fitness. In 1 Timothy 4:8, we read: "For physical training is of some value, but godliness has value for all things, holding promise for both the present life and the life to come." We should keep our physical bodies in good shape. It is God's temple while we are here on earth; and we can more effectively serve God if we have healthy, fit bodies. So physical training has some value, but it is for a temporal purpose and should be kept in its proper perspective, because the more important aspect of life, the development of our character, is for eternity.

One of my favorite scriptures related to fitness is found in Paul's letter to the Philippians. "For, as I have often told you before and now say again even with tears, many live as enemies of the cross of Christ. Their destiny is destruction, their god is their stomach, and their glory is in their shame" (Philippians 3:18-19). THEIR GOD IS THEIR STOMACH! Most people are much more concerned about filling their stomach than their spirit. I'm not referring to persons dying of hunger. The filling of the stomach becomes an obsession with the majority of the people in our society-even though it is very unlikely that anyone will starve to death.

Sometime take note of television commercials and count the number of spots that are selling either grooming items (toothpaste, hair conditioners, makeup, etc.) or food and beverages. Advertisers are very smart people. They know what appeals to the public. If they can appeal to us either through our appearance (i.e. American society's standard of appearance) or our stomachs, they are going to sell products.

In an earlier chapter we discussed Paul's "thorn" as recorded in the 12th Chapter of 2 Corinthians, and noted that the recorded reason for the thorn was to keep Paul from becoming conceited or prideful. What that "thorn" was is really not known, and it has been conjectured to be everything from poor eyesight to malaria. Whatever it was, it was a physical problem. Three times Paul pleaded with the Lord to take it away, so it must have been something very bothersome and probably affected his appearance in one way or another. Even if pain is the result of an internal problem, it is reflected in our outward appearance. A physical problem that continually torments a person is inevitably reflected in his appearance. We might learn two things from Paul here. First, if we have a physical problem that we can do something about with the Lord's help, we should ask him for the power to do it (for example: lose weight, require less sleep, have more energy, heal an affliction, keep our bodies cleaner, be better groomed, etc.); and secondly, if we ask the Lord repeatedly and earnestly for this help and He chooses not to take that thorn away, it may well be that the Lord is leaving us with that blemish so that we learn that God's grace is sufficient, and our inner being is more important to develop!

Although Peter is talking about women in the following reference, the principle is there for all to learn. "Your beauty should not come from outward adornment, such as braided hair and the wearing of gold jewelry and fine clothes. Instead, it should be that of your inner self, the unfading beauty of a gentle and quiet spirit, which is a great worth in God's sight" (1 Peter 3:3-4).

We can probably all think of examples of people who represent both ends of this spectrum. At one end of the spectrum is the beautiful woman who smells nice, wears nice clothing and jewelry, always has her hair nicely done, and really makes a striking appearance. But when you get to really know that person, her character, her values, etc., the external beauty often fades. At the other end of the spectrum is the woman who dresses neatly but not fancy, wears little makeup but has a very sweet, loving inner being. Of course, it could be reversed. The more attractive woman could also be the one with the beautiful inner character! We use women here only as an example. The same idea could be applied to men. It doesn't take long for us to see what a person is really like. And, of course, God can see through our superficiality immediately. He knows our inner character and the gentle, loving and quiet spirit is great in His sight. That is what we ought to be concentrating on in our character development. Remember, Paul said that keeping the body fit and looking good has SOME value, but our spiritual growth is of surpassing value. Paul repeats this theme in his first letter to Timothy. "I also want women to dress modestly, with decency and propriety, not with braided hair or gold or pearls or expensive clothes . . ." (1 Timothy 2:9).

James uses physical appearance to illustrate another important point relating to appearance. "Anyone who listens to the Word but does not do what it says is like a man who looks at his face in a mirror and, after looking at himself, goes away and immediately forgets what he looks like" (James 1:23-24). This sounds like a problem we also have today. People go to church and to Bible studies and hear the Word, then go away and don't apply anything they heard! In the days of James, mirrors were not mercury- coated glass, rather they were made of polished metal. People would look into these mirrors and see their ruffled appearance, then go away and do nothing about it. He was comparing that behavior of a ruffled appearance soon forgotten, to soon forgetting the heard Word.

It is so easy to fall into the human trap of making value judgments on first impressions. Have you ever noticed how easy it is to want to get to know someone who has a nice appearance. In fact, it is much easier to love someone who has a nice appearance because that first impression of looks, from an earthly viewpoint, is desirable! It is more difficult to get to know someone who is not particularly attractive physically because the inner being, the quiet, humble, gentle spirit, which is of great worth in God's sight, is not necessarily represented by that outward physical beauty-which temporarily attracts.

A final contributing factor to one's appearance that warrants consideration is what comes out of the mouth in the form of speech. Often a person has all the attributes of a beautiful person outwardly, but that beauty is often made ugly by the kind of talk that comes out of their mouths. Pride, arrogance, haughtiness, or whatever word you wish to use to describe the sin, originates in the heart but is expressed primarily by the mouth. Pride can certainly be manifested by how we walk, by the expressions on our face, and by other forms of non-verbal communication; however, our inner being is primarily reflected by what comes out of our mouths. "Likewise the tongue is a small part of the body, but it makes great boasts. Consider what a great forest is set on fire by a small spark. The tongue also is a fire, a world of evil among the parts of the body. It corrupts the whole person, sets the whole course of his life on fire, and is itself set on fire by hell." (James 3:5-6) With the tongue we praise our lord, curse others, and make great boasts! This should not be! One out of three is sufficient if it is the right one. We should constantly praise the Lord, recognizing Him as our source and the source of all our attributes. But we should not use the mouth to curse or speak evil of others or to boast of our "own" nice appearance. "Let another praise you, and not your own mouth; someone else, and not your own lips." (Proverbs: 27:2)

There is an expression that has been around for centuries—"cleanliness is next to Godliness." There is no scriptural reference for this statement. It probably originated from "all mothers" since almost all mothers have told their children that "proverb" many times! The scriptures seem to be quite clear that we are to keep our physical bodies in good shape, to look nice, be clean, and to control our speech, all of which reflect on our "appearance". We are also taught in the scriptures that we are not to dwell on our appearance or use it as a source of pride; rather, we are commissioned to concentrate on developing a humble, loving, quiet spirit.

FATHER IN HEAVEN, IT IS SO EASY FOR US TO BE PROUD OF OUR ACCOMPLISHMENTS AND FOR SOME TO BE PROUD OF THEIR GOOD LOOKS, FINE CLOTHES, GOOD HEALTH AND FANCY JEWELRY. FATHER WE KNOW THAT THESE MERELY GIVE A SUPERFICIAL LOOK AT WHAT WE REALLY ARE LIKE AND SOMETIMES HOW WE ARE TRYING TO FAKE IT IN LIFE, OR ARE TRYING TO BE OR LOOK LIKE SOMETHING WE ARE NOT. HELP US, FATHER, TO FOLLOW YOUR WORD, HELP US TO TAKE PROPER CARE OF THE TEMPLE YOU HAVE GIVEN US, TO VALUE IT, BUT YET NOT BE POSSESSED BY IT. HELP US TO REALIZE THAT ALL WE POSSESS WE HAVE BEEN GIVEN BY YOU AND THAT WHAT WE HAVE IS SUFFICIENT. KEEP US FROM BOASTING, FATHER, AND HELP US TO DEVELOP OUR INNER CHARACTER SO THAT WE MIGHT BECOME MORE LIKE YOUR SON. IN HIS NAME WE PRAY. AMEN

CHAPTER 9

Pride in Our Status or Position

Pride often becomes a problem when a person has obtained a position that has some prominence or authority. It seems to be closely related to another problem man has-his inability to deal with power. Have you ever heard a person boast about the position they hold in local government, or in the business community, or in the educational system, or (heaven forbid) in the church you attend? Perhaps you've encountered a "professional" person, such as a physician, lawyer, or professor who has quite an elevated opinion of him/herself as a result of the position they hold, or their perceived importance of their accomplishments? They may not come right out and say they are superior, rather it's more often a subtle sophistication that permeates their personality. This sin is not found only in professional, but in persons in all walks of life. I have seen men who have been promoted to supervisor of a group of janitors become so filled with pride that they become very difficult to work with. Many people let a little power or authority "go to their head". This seems to be a universal human trait. It can be seen in any society, regardless of the development of that society. It occurs in third world nations, jungle tribes, and our most "developed" or sophisticated societies.

Often, when people are successful in business and/or finance, they look for another challenge. That challenge is usually a position that entails a certain amount of power. Unfortunately, this has proven to be true with many of our leaders in government. Being in a position of leadership or being very successful does not necessarily mean that a person will inevitably be filled with pride; but, more often than not, that is the case. Persons in a position of power, which dictates making decisions affecting the lives of people, very easily succumb to the sin of pride. Government leaders often become so proud they begin to think they are above the law and, yes, often because of their great power, come to believe they are God! Unfortunately, this occasionally occurs in religious sects also. The Jim Jones tragedy was the result of a human who became so powerful and prideful that he convinced hundreds of people that he was God. He had such power over his followers that he even convinced most of them to take their own lives! We could go on and on naming leaders in America, and in almost all other countries in the world, who became so proud that they felt themselves to be above ANY law of man or God. As a result, they were or will be eventually thrown down from power just as Satan was. The Bible tells a great deal about this sin. There are many examples for us in the Old and New Testaments that teach us how we ought to handle power, the result of forgetting God when we reach positions of high status; and, also, the blessings we and those "under us" can realize if we are humble and God fearing people.

Uzziah was one of the Kings of Judah. He became King at the early age of sixteen and reigned over Jerusalem for 52 years. He started out his kingship doing what was right in the sight of the Lord. As long as he sought the Lord, God gave him success. He built many things in and around Jerusalem, acquired much livestock, developed agriculture, developed a large and well-equipped army that was very successful in battle against the Philistines, Arabs of Gur Baal, and the Meunites. "His fame spread far and wide, for he was greatly helped until he became powerful. But after Uzziah became powerful, his pride led to his downfall. He was unfaithful to the Lord his God . . ." (2 Chronicles 26:15-16) Uzziah became so enamored with the success he was having that he soon came to believe that it was all his own doing and he didn't need God because he was doing such a great job by himself! All of the sudden Uzziah contracted leprosy! He lived the rest of his life isolated in a house.

Not too long after King Uzzian's reign, Hezekiah became King. Hezekiah was 25 when he became king, and he reigned in Jerusalem for 29 years. Hezekiah did many great things. He did what was right and faithful before the Lord. "In everything that he undertook in the service of God's temple and in obedience to the law and the commands, he sought his God and worked wholeheartedly. And so he prospered." (2 Chronicles 31:21) Sennacherib, King of Assyria, was at the same time making plans to invade Judah. When the word of this attack became widespread and the people had reason to fear a great army, Hezekiah said: "'Do not be afraid or discouraged because of the king of Assyria and the vast army with him, for there is a greater power with us than with him. With him is only the arm of flesh, but with us is the Lord our God to help us and to fight our battles.' And the people gained confidence from what Hezekiah the king of Judah said." (2 Chronicles 32:7-8) With the Lord's help the army of Hezekiah defeated King Sennacherib and his great army; and, from then on, Hezekiah was highly regarded by all nations. Can you guess what happened then? "But Hezekiah's heart was proud and he did not respond to the kindness shown him; therefore the Lord's wrath was on him and on Judah and Jerusalem." (2 Chronicles 32:25) Hezekiah became so powerful with God's help that he decided he would try leading without his reliance on God.

Maybe after his loss of power he remembered about the fate
of Uzziah and wondered if the reason things were not going
too well was because of his own pride! We do know from
the Word (2 Chronicles 32:26), however, that for some reason Hezekiah repented of the pride of his heart and so did
the people of Jerusalem who were his followers. As a result
of their repentance, Jerusalem continued to prosper during
the days of Hezekiah.

Hezekiah's son, Manasseh, followed his father as king.
In Chapter 33 of 2 Chronicles we read of all the atrocious
things Manasseh did and how, because of his sins, the
enemy was allowed to take him prisoner, put a hook in his
nose, shackle him and whisk him off to Babylon. In his dis-
tress, Manasseh repented, sought the favor of the Lord his
God, HUMBLED HIMSELF greatly before the God of his
fathers, and was restored to power. Amon, Manasseh's son,
did many evil things just as his father did before him, but
unlike his father, Amon did not repent. He refused to humble himself before the Lord because he had such great power
that he just did not believe he needed any God to tell him
what to do! He had the power to do anything himself! He
reigned only two years before he was assassinated.

Another young king of Judah named Zedekiah fell into
the same trap, that is, he became so powerful and filled with
pride that he would not recognize God. "He did evil in the
eyes of the Lord his God and did not humble himself before
Jeremiah the prophet, who spoke the word of the Lord." (2
Chronicles 36:12). ". . .He became stiff-necked and hardened his heart and would not turn to the Lord, the God of
Israel." (2 Chronicles 36:13) Zedekiah not only would not
humble himself before God, he lead his people in outright
rebellion against God. The people would not listen to God's
messengers, despised his words and scoffed at his prophets
to such an extent that God took action against all of them.
Because they would not humble themselves, they lost all

"But when his heart became arrogant and hardened with pride, he was deposed from his royal throne and stripped of his glory. He was driven away from his people and given the mind of an animal; he lived with the wild donkeys and ate grass like cattle; and his body was drenched with the dew of heaven, until he acknowledged that the Most High God is sovereign over the kingdoms of men and sets over them anyone he wishes."
Daniel 5:20-21

their material possessions, the lives of their young men and women, treasures of the temple and of the kings, and so on. All remaining people and loot were carried off to Babylon. The temple was set on fire, the walls of Jerusalem were broken down, and Judah lay desolate simply because this young king felt so powerful that he believed he and his kingdom could do anything WITHOUT GOD.

The pagan king of Babylon named Nebuchadnezzar was in power at the time, doing what one would expect a pagan king to do—constructing large idols of gold, practicing astrology, and so on. Nebuchadnezzar became very powerful, contented, and prosperous; and, you guessed it, hardened with pride. But one night he had a dream that disturbed him greatly, and it was a dream he could not understand. So he called his magicians, enchanter, astrologers and diviners to interpret the dream, but they could not understand it either. So Daniel, the young Israelite, was called upon to interpret the dream, and he told Nebuchadnezzar precisely what it meant. Sure enough, a year later all the things Daniel explained about the dream came to pass. A voice came from heaven and said: "This is what is decreed for you, King Nebuchadnezzar: Your royal authority has been taken from you. You will be driven away from people and will live with the wild animals; you will eat grass like cattle. Seven times will pass by for you until you acknowledge that the Most High is sovereign over the kingdoms of men and gives them to anyone he wishes." (Daniel 4:31-33) Nebuchadnezzar was very "hard headed"! He was a great king deposed of his throne and destined to live in the fields like an animal FOR SEVEN YEARS before he finally humbled himself before God. Nebuchadnezzar raised his eyes toward heaven, praised the Most High, and honored and glorified God. He acknowledged that everything God does is just and right and ". . . those who walk in pride he is able to humble" (Daniel 4:37). It took a long time for this king to acknowledge God, but he did learn the lesson—the "hard way". If Nebuchadnezzar lived today, his testimony about God's ability to humble any man would qualify him as an "expert witness". He knew what it was to be a great and proud king, to be humbled like the lowly animals; and, in the end, to repent and acknowledge God's power!

Unfortunately, this is a very difficult lesson for men to learn, and it must be relearned every generation. His own son, Belshazzar, who succeeded him on the throne, refused to humble himself, knowing full well the story of his father's life. He set himself up proudly against the Lord of heaven, but just a short time later, he was assassinated. We see this pattern repeated over and over in Old Testament times. Some rulers, those who humbled themselves before God, were good kings who feared God; and their nations prospered. We also see some kings who followed God until they were successful and powerful and then rejected God because they no longer needed Him. These men were destroyed along with their nations. Then we also have examples of the ruler who relied on God, became powerful, fell into the sin of pride and lost everything, but repented and was restored to his kingship.

These examples of men in powerful positions are from the Old Testament, but are by no means exclusive to that era. The lust for power and the resultant pride occurs all throughout history. Even today we see leaders who become so filled with pride that they believe they do not need to humble themselves before God. Their fate is no different than hundreds of their predecessors'. WHY DOESN'T MAN LEARN FROM HISTORY? If we are in a position of power, we should humble ourselves and acknowledge that wherever we are, we are there by the grace of God; and, therefore, we should serve with the strength God provides, so that in all things God may be praised through Jesus Christ. (1 Peter 4:11 paraphrased) AMEN.

Today in America, we have our Watergates, Enron scams and many other kinds of political problems related to the sin of pride. But, don't let anyone ever convince you this is a unique problem to America. It is a problem faced by all of mankind all over the world! It is particularly upsetting in America, because so many of us are still naïve enough to think of our country as a "moral Christian democracy". We expect our leaders to place America and its people before their personal gains. Not so in many cases! With regard to the rest of the world, we simply do not hear much about the corruption in other countries where there is not a free press, and the people are oppressed. For example, there are countries where it is not unusual for a person in power to simply imprison or eliminate political opposition! Even if there is an "election" it is rather difficult to campaign if you and all your supporters are in prison! Yes! Pride leading to power and corruption is everywhere in man's world.

Thus far we have been primarily emphasizing the problem of pride as it relates to persons in high places or to people of "high status"—specifically in government. This game, or struggle for power, is evident at all levels of the political spectrum—in local, state and national governments. It seems as though the degree to which we fall captive to the sin of pride may be directly proportional to our status, or the amount of influence we have over other people. God does indeed hate pride! "He humbles those who dwell on high, he lays the lofty city low." (Isaiah 26:5) ". . .he has scattered those who are proud in their inmost thoughts. He has brought down rulers from their thrones but has lifted up the humble." (Luke 1:51-52) You may be thinking at this point-"wait a moment, I know of many people who are filled with pride and they are, in fact, very successful!" This, at a first glance, may appear to be a contradiction to what we are told in the Bible. Why is not everyone who is proud brought down in humility? God's Word also tells about these people. Job tells us that even if on occasion a leader becomes powerful and prideful and is not humbled by God, he 1) may yet be humbled at a later time, and 2) he will definitely be held accountable for his conduct at the day of judgment. "But God drags away the mighty by his power; though they become established, they have no assurance of life." (Job 24:22) So we may, in fact, be proudly successful in this life! The same teaching is given in Psalm 73. Here we are given the picture of the person who seems to be doing everything that is contrary to God's teaching, and they seem to be very successful. Yet, they are consumed by pride. After enumerating all the ramifications of this "successful" person, the author says: "When I tried to understand all this, it was oppressive to me till I entered the sanctuary of God; THEN I UNDERSTOOD THEIR FINAL DESTINY." (Psalm 73:16-17) We often tend to believe that, in order for God's justice to prevail, we have to see it now! Not true! This may be man's logic, but it is not God's! We MAY see and understand the fate of people whose lives have been dominated by pride when we enter the sanctuary; and on the other hand, maybe we won't.

This problem of pride of position can be seen in nearly all walks of ordinary life in addition to the political scene. We sometimes see it in the family, where the head of the family "lords his authority" over his family in an unloving manner. He unjustly makes arbitrary decisions solely on his authority of power or position as head of the family. In our position of employment, we always have to submit to a supervisor unless we are "the head man". These positions of leadership can be held by persons who are compassionate, understanding and helpful, or they can be held by tyrants. The tyrant is often a person so filled with pride because of their accomplishments and attainment of their high status that power "goes to their head" and they begin to wear the cloak of arrogance. In order to further justify their place of dominance they often tend to

take advantage of the weak or mild personality. In denomina-
tional churches there are often organized political strategies
planned for power struggles by opposing factions. Pride often
becomes a real problem when appointments are made for
deacons, elders, bishops and so on. In the local church, the
pastor can have such great success in building a large congregation that he becomes very prideful.

These are just a few examples of the many instances
where people who are in leadership positions have the potential of becoming arrogant and proud. Of course, we don't have
to be that way. Just as in the days of the kings of Judah, we,
today, have the ability to choose to be humble. We can look to
the Lord for our strength and recognize Him as the source of
our success, or we can reject the Lord and claim that our MD
or PH.D degree, our position as department head, our position
as chief engineer, our role as a pastor in a growing congregation of believers, and so on, is solely a product of our own
hard work! This attitude is precisely that which the religion of
humanism holds. Man does not need a deity-he can do it on
his own! THIS IS WHAT GOD HATES! "In his arrogance the
wicked man hunts down the weak, who are caught in the
schemes he devises." (Psalm 10:2).

If we choose to humbly bow before God and rely on
him for all our needs, we can hold positions of power, status, or authority with great success. The Psalmist tells us:
"In your majesty ride forth victoriously in behalf of truth,
humility and righteousness." (Psalm 45:4) David was a
great king and said: "For you have been my hope, O
Sovereign Lord, my confidence since my youth. From birth
I have relied on you. . ." (Psalm 71:5-6) The apostle Paul
pleaded with God to remove the thorn from his side, but the
Lord said to Paul: "My grace is sufficient for you, for my
power is made perfect in weakness . . ." (2 Corinthians
12:9). The temptation to be filled with pride is so powerful
that we need a constant reminder, as Paul did, to tell us that

our power is made perfect in our weakness-that is, if we are constantly reminded that we can do nothing on our own power, we will be wanting to constantly look to the Lord as the source and power to do all things, and when we do that we will be a powerful witness to the Christian life. This is what God wants. He wants us to be in constant communication-especially when we are in positions of high status and/or power! We know that the Lord will bless us in that position if we look to Him, and that this humility will be taken into consideration at the day of judgment. "When a wicked man dies, his hope perishes; all he expected from his power comes to nothing." (Proverbs 11:7) ". . .If anyone serves, he should do it with the strength God provides, so that in all things God may be praised through Jesus Christ." (1 Peter 4:11) What a different world we could have if people holding positions of status or power would constantly praise God and look to Him, rather than trying to do it on their own and reveling in pride over what they see to be their own accomplishments.

FATHER IN HEAVEN, WE PRAY THAT YOU WILL GIVE US HUMILITY. WE PRAY THAT YOU WILL PRO-TECT US FROM THE SIN OF PRIDE-PARTICULARLY THOSE IN A POSITION OF POWER IN SOCIETY, AND FOR THOSE WHO HAVE OBTAINED HIGH STATUS IN THEIR SOCIETY. FATHER, WE CAN SEE FROM YOUR WORD THAT YOU WILL BLESS US IF WE USE OUR POSITION IN LIFE, REGARDLESS OF STATUS, FOR YOUR GLORY; AND WE PRAY THAT WE WILL CON-STANTLY LOOK TO YOU AS OUR SOURCE IN MAK-ING EVEN THE SMALLEST DECISION THAT AFFECTS OTHER PEOPLE. HELP US TO BE LOVING AND CARING AND TO RESPECT THOSE UNDER OUR CARE AS YOUR CHILDREN. IN JESUS' NAME WE PRAY. AMEN.

CHAPTER 10

Pride in Our Children

One of the most commonly seen forms of human pride is that exhibited by parents over their children. Parents seem to have an innate desire to constantly tell others how great their kids are. In fact, it often occurs within the first few days after birth! Have you ever seen or heard parents suggest that because their new baby was very long at birth it must be going to be a tall person! Wow, he has such long fingers maybe he is going to be a good pianist, and so on. This innate desire to have pride in one's children continues, actually to death. I have heard people in their eighties and above brag about their 60 year old "children".

Probably the reason most parents have a "natural" tendency to exhibit great pride in their children (in addition to the fact that they love them so much) is the fact that THEY created them. A physical act between the parents created the zygote (the fertilized egg) that eventually became a living human being; which, in a sense, becomes a living extension of themselves. Anyone who has witnessed the miracle of birth and has reflected on the process can't help but be amazed at the process that enables this single cell to develop into a living human being. Then, in a mere couple of years that entity is walking, running, thinking, talking, and "on and on". Before we look into God's Word on this matter, let's recall a few more common examples of how we tend to show pride in our children.

Often, when visiting friends and relatives, we inquire about the well-being of their children in order to learn what they are doing, how they are doing, where they are, and so on, as a matter of genuine interest. On the other hand, parents often initiate a conversation that will eventually allow them to brag about their own children. This usually comes about because the parent has a great deal of personal pride in their children, and/or they have no other interests to talk about! Have you ever heard parents boast about how well their children are doing in school? "Henry is at the top of his high school class and has had scholarship offers from 10 of the leading colleges in the country!" "Susie got the highest mark on a test the other day!" Or occasionally one hears something like this: "Joanie is really a smart kid even though she is not at the top of the class-she just doesn't get along with her teacher very well!" Today, with our "high tech" society introducing home computers to young preschool children, we hear parents boasting about how their children know the alphabet and all kinds of other things, as a result of "playing" on the home computer. Most parents would like to think their children are a bit precocious—at least in some areas!

How about the area of sport! Have you ever heard a parent boast of the athletic prowess of their children? Wow! We probably hear this type of boasting by parents more often than we hear boasting about academic success or intelligence! This fact, of course, mirrors our society. The great athlete is more highly respected in society (in general) than the intellectual or the individual who has their spiritual life in good order! Kids certainly get more recognition and acceptance by their peers as a result of their participation in sports than their academic achievements. The next time you attend a school or community athletic contest take a good philosophical look at the parents of the kids participating. How are they reacting? How are the parents whose kids are on the team, but not playing, reacting?

There are numerous other reasons why parents brag about their offspring—physical size, character, being popular with their peers, being popular with the opposite sex, being helpful around the house, having other talents such as music ability, and so on.

About now you may be ready to throw a brick my way, or say: "What's with this guy? These are normal reactions of parents; and, in no way, should they be related to the sin of pride!" Before we look to God's Word, bear with me a little bit longer. Let's examine a few possible reasons for secular man having pride in his children. Earlier in this chapter the conception of the child was briefly mentioned as a uniting of the sperm and egg to form a zygote. Pride is initiated even here when parents realize they have the power to create a new human being. This ability to create is, in itself, a miracle that can lead some to believe that, if they did indeed create it, it must be good. Therefore, it becomes an object of our pride. This act also gives us the potential to make this new creature into something we have not been able to attain or could never be! It is, for many people, the opportunity to fulfill their aspirations through their offspring. We want our children to be what we could never be, but what we would like to be! Because they are genetically an extension of our lives, our great potential (which we have been unable to develop for one reason or another) might come to fruition in our progeny. So our own pride is fed by boasting of the accomplishments of our son or daughter.

A good example of this may be seen by analyzing the thinking of a close friend of mine who has, as yet, not seen the need of accepting Christ into his life. He has a very fine family. He has a lovely wife, and they have conceived and

"Love is patient, love is kind. It does not envy,
it does not boast, it is not proud."
1 Corinthians 13:4

raised two beautiful daughters without the help of anyone, or anything—certainly not the help of the Lord. He is very proud of his family, and believes he has done it all. Who needs God! I believe his pride is the greatest barrier to his coming to know Christ. His children have attained things in life that he has been unable to accomplish, and through their accomplishments he has become very proud!

The key to the understanding of pride in our children is a matter of attitude. Remember, the basis for pride is the human "necessity" of building up our own ego-the "I did it" or "I can do it by myself" attitude. The Bible has a great deal to say regarding the raising of children, and many books have been written on that topic. Surprisingly, little is directly said in the scriptures about pride in our children. However, most of the teaching on pride can be applied to the examination of the pride we have in our children. Let's look at Jacob's response to his brother Essau (whom he had not seen for many years) when Essau said: "who are these with you?" Jacob answered, "they are the children God has graciously given your servant". (Genesis 33:5) Isaiah declares: "Here am I, and the children the Lord has given me". (Isaiah 8:18) What a completely different attitude we might have, as Christians, toward our children and their accomplishments (or even their lack of accomplishments!) if we acknowledge that they are a gracious gift from God. Another key scripture that helps us understand this teaching is found in Proverbs: "The father of a righteous man has great joy; he who has a wise son delights in him. May your father and mother be glad; may she who gave you birth rejoice!" (Proverbs 23:24-25) Nowhere in the Bible do we find any teaching that says: be proud of your children! Rather, we are told to take great joy, be glad, and rejoice in our children because they are a gift from God! Can you see the big difference between the two attitudes? The prideful person is ego-centered or self-centered; whereas, the Christian attitude should be Christ centered. The prideful person says: "I conceived the child. I gave him his great intellectual ability. I gave him his great athletic or musical ability. What I have not been able to accomplish because of my "hard luck", my progeny will (should) accomplish." The Christian, on the other hand, if they look upon their children as a gift from God, see the talents of their children as gifts God has bestowed upon them and rejoice and praise God for those kids and their abilities, whatever they may be!

What a great witness we could have as Christians, if we would only be more careful how we express out feelings. Of course, those feelings should be genuine and from the heart. If we expressed our joy in the gift God has given us when our children do something well and give God the glory, it would not only witness to others as to our source, but also indicate that we are not taking credit for their talents. Of course, some of the gifts we have been given from God are genetically transmitted to our children; but we can't take credit for them either, since they were a gift from God through our parents. Remember what James taught us: "Likewise the tongue is a small part of the body, but it makes great boasts. (James 3:5) When we boast about our children (ourselves, indirectly), those who hear know to whom we are giving credit!

Helping our children to understand the issue of self pride is also important. Certainly we should praise our children when they do things well, just as we should reprimand them when they do things wrong. But while doing so, we must also teach them the delicate difference between self-reliance and reliance on God. As we love and bring up our children, Paul gives us some words of wisdom on which to reflect in his letter to the Corinthians. "Love is patient, love is kind. It does not envy, it does not boast, it is not proud. It is not rude, it is not self-seeking, it is not easily angered, it keeps no record of wrongs. Love does not delight in evil but rejoices with the truth". (1 Corinthians 13:4-6) We can show evidence of our love and joy in our children by rejoicing in the truth and teaching them the truth. That is, that OUR KIDS AND THEIR TALENTS ARE GIFTS FROM GOD. Also notice the phrase "love is not self-seeking"! We should give love and rejoice in what God has given us, because God first loved us, not for what we will get as a result and not for self gratification, which is the root of pride!

Sometimes adults deal with their children's potential for building their own pride by having many children. The reasoning may go something like this: "The more boys I have the greater the chance that one will become a great athlete." That wise man of old, Solomon, teaches us a great lesson about pride in our children in respect to numbers. Solomon said that a man could have a hundred children and live many years; yet no matter how long he lives ... without God and the keeping of His commandments, all is vanity-a chasing after the wind. (Ecclesiastes 6:3, 12:13 paraphrased)

Solomon's teaching leads us to the essence of what we should have joy in and rejoice about. Certainly we should rejoice in most things, but the Bible gives a command that we should raise our children in the Lord and tells us of the promise of prosperity if we do! "These commandments that I give you today are to be upon your hearts. Impress them on your children. Talk about them when you sit at home and when you walk along the road, when you lie down and when you get up. Tie them as symbols on your hands and bind them on your foreheads. Write them on the doorframes of your house and on your gates". (Deuteronomy 6:6-9) That teaching sounds like we are committed to teach our children the way of the Lord at all times-wherever we are! Lest one feel that this is "Old Testament Law", from which we are now free, look at what Paul teaches: "Fathers, do not exasperate your children; instead, bring them up in the training and instruction of the Lord." (Ephesians 6:4) Moses also tells us of the promise of doing so. "And when you and your children return to the Lord your God and obey him with all your heart and with all your soul according to everything I command you today, then the Lord your God will restore your fortunes and have compassion on you. . ." (Deuteronomy 30:2-3) So our joy and rejoicing in our children should be in raising them in God's Word and leading them into salvation.

What greater joy could parents have than in knowing that their children have made a commitment to Jesus Christ. As David said: "But I trust in your unfailing love; my heart rejoices in your salvation." (Psalm 13:5) Isaiah, in his prophesy of how men will praise the Lord, said: "This is the Lord, we trusted in him; let us rejoice and be glad in his salvation". (Isaiah 25:9) God's Word plainly teaches us that we should rejoice in our salvation and in our children's salvation-not being proud; rather, rejoicing that by God's grace our children have been saved.

As humans, it is a real temptation to brag or boast about our children. God, however, wants us to keep our sight on Him at all times. Rather than boasting of our kids' accomplishments or attributes, which is an ego or self-gratifying thing, we should be grateful, joyful, and rejoice that the Lord has given our children to us. Whatever gifts they have are from Him, and we should praise God continually for our children-whatever their gifts may be. If we are to be proud of our children, it should be in relation to what Paul taught in 2 Corinthians. That is, if we must boast, boast in the Lord and boast in your brothers and sisters in Christ. In that sense, if we have any right to boast at all about our children, it is that they know Jesus Christ as their Lord and Savior.

FATHER IN HEAVEN, THIS IS A VERY HARD LESSON FOR US TO LEARN. WE JUST SEEM TO WANT TO BOAST ABOUT A LOT OF THINGS TO BUILD UP

OUR OWN EGO, AND THIS IS ESPECIALLY TRUE WHEN IT COMES TO OUR CHILDREN. LORD HELP US TO REALIZE THAT OUR CHILDREN ARE A GIFT FROM YOU, AND WE ARE TO CHERISH THIS GIFT. HELP US TO REALIZE THAT THE TALENTS AND GIFTS THEY HAVE ARE NOT BY OUR DOING. RATHER, THEY ARE FROM YOU. HELP US TO REMEMBER TO PRAISE YOU FOR THOSE GIFTS AND SHOW OUR JOY AND APPRECIATION OUT-WARDLY IN A LOVING WAY. LORD WE PRAY THAT IN REJOICING IN OUR CHILDREN YOU WILL BE PRAISED. IN THE NAME OF JESUS CHRIST WE PRAY. AMEN

CHAPTER 11

Pride in Achievements

From our earliest years, most of us can remember our parents telling us that we should make the most of our lives and attempt to reach our maximum potential. In fact, in America, as well as in almost all other cultures, children are taught to be "high achievers". "Be a success at whatever you do!" is a commonly heard expression. There are problems associated with this basic philosophy, of course. For example, we can ask the classical questions—What is success? Is achievement an end in itself and the object of achievement inconsequential? What things have a place of high value and are thus worthy of achieving? Are these worthy values universal for mankind, or are they relative to the culture in which one is living? Do worthy values fluctuate depending on one's situation? Should Christians "rest" in their salvation? As Americans, we have been continually bombarded in educational institutions to value high achievement. Probably everyone would agree with this thought, if we could agree as to what is worthy of achieving!

Because being a high achiever is generally held as a worthy value in America, and because rewards are usually associated with high achievement, those who are rewarded for their success tend to be very proud people. Popular literature abounds with stories of poor children growing up to be successful millionaires. Those stories usually include statements, or at least implications that go something like: "I pulled myself up out of the gutter and became successful. Anyone else with enough ambition and willingness to work hard can do the same!"

The Christian must carefully and continually seek the answer to the question—What in life has high value? That is, what is worthy for me to aspire to and to encourage my children to attain? Our schools teach a few basic values that, at first glance, may seem to be worthy—such as knowledge. You may be saying to yourself: Wouldn't anyone believe that knowledge is worthy? The obvious response to this question is knowledge in what—man's wisdom or God's wisdom? That thought could be expanded to say that a "good education" has value. One problem here is that many individuals believe that "good" is synonymous with the amount of education one has. Do you have a high school diploma? A college bachelor of arts degree? A master's degree, an M.D. degree, a Ph.D. degree, post-doctoral work? Have you ever observed a correlation between the amount of pride an individual has and the amount of education they have? The degree one has says nothing about the quality of the education received. What a "good" education is would need to be examined.

A related attainment holding high value in American society is the acquirement of material things. Having a lot of material things is a sign of success! In fact, success is thought by many people to be proportional to the amount of material things one has accumulated. It is difficult to acquire a lot of material things without being a high achiever (unless, of course, you inherit them).

People can be high achievers in anything they do. The homemaker can be the best there is! The garbage collector can be the best in the business! The factory supervisor can

"Everyone who competes in the games goes into strict training. They do it to get a crown that will not last; but we do it
to get a crown that will last forever."
1 Corinthians 9:25

be the best in the plant! The student can be the best scholar in the class! The minister can be the best preacher! The athlete can be the best in the school, district or state! The Sunday school teacher can be the best in the church! Again, if you carefully think of people who fulfill these stations in life, you usually see a high correlation between their success and their pride. I'm ready to get hit by the thrown brick again-I know! You must be thinking "what's wrong with taking pride in a job well done"? It all boils down to MOTIVE. Why do you want to be the best homemaker, garbage collector, supervisor, student, athlete, teacher, etc.? To show the world how far you have gone!-or how well YOU have done? Is it for your own glory or is it your desire to achieve to the best of your ability for the purpose of glorifying God-who gave you the ability? If the latter is true, do you really glorify God publicly or privately each time you accomplish something? Look at what the apostle John says. "For everything in the world-the cravings of sinful man, the lust of his eyes and the boasting of what he has and does-comes not from the Father but from the world". (1 John 2:16) Wow! How much more to the point could we get. Generally we are more interested in impressing our fellow men with our achievements than pleasing our Lord and God! If that is true, we must question what our god really is-is it man or God? It can't be both! Christ said: "How can you believe if you accept praise from one another, yet make no effort to obtain the praise that comes from the only God!" (John 5:44) Verdict? We are guilty! It is really heartwarming to see a prominent public figure (sports figures, for example) thank God first and foremost for their accomplishment-in public and often on national TV!

Looking into the word for examples of high achievers leads us to several very popular personalities. In discussing human achievements we must examine the life of Solomon. God gave Solomon a wise and discerning heart that was greater than any before and greater than any after him. Solomon knew about biology, zoology, philosophy, and wrote thousands of proverbs. He was a great builder, having built the temple in Jerusalem and his own palace, which took thirteen years to build. He also built and rebuilt cities in Jerusalem, Lebanon, and many other places. Every year Solomon received the equivalent of over four million dollars in gold as mere tribute from neighboring kings. He had fleets of ships, fourteen hundred chariots and twelve thousand horses. Solomon had seven hundred wives and three hundred concubines! Was Solomon successful? Did he achieve very much? By earthly standards Solomon had EVERYTING! He had wisdom, wealth, possessions, women, armies-you name it and Solomon had it! His dad, King David, probably would have rejoiced in his son—for a while. David told Solomon, just before his death, to "observe what the Lord your God requires: Walk in his ways, and keep his decrees and commands, his laws and requirements, as written in the Law of Moses, so that you may prosper in all you do and wherever you go." (1 Kings 2:3) Solomon followed God's law and prospered greatly; then, probably because of his great success, pride and feeling of self-sufficiency, broke God's law and, for a time, life lost all meaning. The theme of the book (Ecclesiastes) he left us is that achieving things and acquiring things to glorify ourselves leads to a meaningless life. In all his wisdom, he didn't catch on to this until his later days. He finally wrote: "'Remember your Creator in the days of your youth, before the days of trouble come and the years approach when you will say, 'I find no pleasure in them' . . ." and "Now all has been heard; here is the conclusion of the matter: Fear God and keep his commandments, for this is the whole duty of man." (Ecclesiastes 12:1, 13) His most important contribution to mankind was to warn us not to make the same mistake he did. He said don't blow it; don't glorify yourself; wise up while you are young, and it will save you a lot of misery! Glorify God by keeping His command- ments—this is the essence of life! This is the highest value man can have.

King Nebuchadnezzar was another classic example of someone achieving great things and claiming it was by his own doing. ". . .as the king was walking on the roof of the royal palace of Babylon, he said, "Is not this the great Babylon I have built as the royal residence, by MY mighty power and for the glory of MY majesty?" (Daniel 4:29-30) We have already seen the fate of Nebuchadnezzer. He was so swelled up with pride in his achievements that he actually believed he was God! There are many other examples in the Old and New Testaments where man has fallen into this trap. If we are achieving for our own glory we are doomed to fail- ure eventually. If we are achieving so that Christ can be glo- rified, then we cannot fail.

In the midst of all his troubles, Job was talking to the Lord and said: "Look at every proud man and bring him low, look at every proud man and humble him, crush the wicked where they stand." (Job 40:11-12) The Lord was reminding Job of His power to humble and crush the one who is filled with pride. God has a way of doing the same thing today. Often, when we forget ourselves and become prideful, God has a way of humbling us. Praise God that He cares enough to do that for us occasionally, so that we do not remain filled with pride.

This is a good time to interject my own testimony, for God was gracious enough to humble this servant. The begin- ning of the testimony will appear as though I am boasting, but please remember I am trying to use my story as an exam- ple of how the Lord does discipline those He loves. Although my life was spent in a Christian home and I did a lot of neat Christian things, I did not really accept Jesus Christ as my Lord and Savior until I was 38. Prior to that time, I had accomplished quite a few things. I had a beautiful family, a nice home, a late model car (and a pickup!). I could beat nearly anybody on campus in racquetball. I had jumped the hurdles necessary to obtain a Bachelor's Degree, a Master's Degree and a Ph.D. Degree from a very prestigious university. I had attained the rank of Associate Professor at a major university and received research grants, written several dozen articles for professional journals; and had authored, or co-authored four books. I had become so academic and enamored with my place within the university that the university had, in fact, become my god. Scientific humanism had become my philosophy of life. The university could solve all of our problems! If there was to be peace in the world, the university sociologists would find a way—scientifically! If there was to be economic stability in the country and in the world, the university economists would find the solutions! Biologists, physiologists, pharmacologists and physicians in medical research would solve the world's population and health problems.

One would hate to describe a national tragedy as a blessing; however, in the case of my personal life, God really worked on me and my pride as a result of the problems in the 1969-70 era. As you may recall, for a number of reasons, universities across the nation found themselves in very trying times. The particular university where I was employed was not exempt. In fact, the university (collectively) in which I had placed my highest expectations, collapsed in front of my eyes. It didn't just slowly crumble, it fell with a thundering crash as the university administration proved itself to be inept; there was a violent ideological split among my colleagues on the faculty; the carnal nature of the faculty, in general, was revealed; and any semblance of order in time of trouble was eroded. It became a time of utter despair for me, personally.

One day, in a state of despair and since no one was

expected to show for classes, I got into my car and left town. I drove to another nearby town, parked the car and began wandering up and down the main street. I stopped in front of a Christian book store and decided I might as well go in and see if there was anything there that could possibly be of interest. While browsing, I came upon the Billy Graham book WORLD AFLAME. I bought the book and walked to a nearby park and read it. I had read many books describing the problem of overpopulation, the problems of government, the problems of . . . . . . .on and on and on! This book was so different because, after he described the same problems, he gave the solution. He pointed out the possibility of a new life in Christ, how only God can satisfy, how to receive Christ, and the future kind of life one has when he has accepted Christ.

I made a commitment to Christ that day, and my life has been pointed in a different direction ever since. "Oh what a difference since Jesus passed by!" God isn't through with me yet (far from it, in fact), but His grace has enabled me to get my priorities in their proper order. Pride is still a sin I have to deal with; and, if this book is of no value to anyone else, I shall read it over and over until God's teachings saturate my carnal nature. One of my favorite scriptures is found in Romans 1:22, "Although they claimed to be wise, they became fools." Secular humanists think they are so wise, that they don't need God, that man can do everything on his own! How sad it is to see your colleagues thinking this way! God has a plan for man, and it's not the same plan the university has! By His grace, I am a part of His Kingdom! Praise be to God!

We are so conditioned to seek praise from our peers and from society, in general, that we often forget the teaching of Christ. Christ said: "I do not accept praise from men, but I know you. I know that you do not have the love of God in your hearts. I have come in my Father's name, an you do not accept me; but if someone else comes in his own name, you will accept him. How can you believe if you accept praise from one another, yet make no effort to obtain the praise that comes from the only God?" (John 5:41-44) We are eager to seek the praise of our peers for our accomplishments, but God wants us to do those things that will be worthy in His eyes! If our god is the true God, we should want to please Him more than man. If we are to please God, then our accomplishments should ALL be to His glory. Notice also that Christ said: " . . .yet make NO EFFORT to obtain the praise of God." (John 5:44) Christ evidently knew it was not easy for humans to give God credit for their accomplishments. Because we are so conditioned by our society to attain specific goals, we become self-centered and have to make AN EFFORT to remember from where our abilities come.

A good note on which to conclude this chapter is the teaching of Paul to the Corinthians regarding the duty of an apostle (and any Christian!): "Everyone who competes in the games goes into strict training. They do it to get a crown that will not last; but we do it to get a crown that will last forever." (1 Corinthians 9:25) We need to train ourselves to thank and praise God each time we accomplish something; and, thereby, acknowledge that our abilities come from Him. Often, in Christian circles, we encounter the person who is completely resting in God's grace. By this, I mean the person who is resting so completely he/she is doing nothing! God gives us all gifts of varying kinds, but he will never force us to use them. He expects us to make an effort to use them, regardless of whether they apply to our jobs or our Christian growth! We have a responsibility to use our God-given talents to their fullest and glorify God in the process. Lazy Christians, who use resting in God's gracc as an excuse for not wanting to grow, will have to answer to their creator one day! In striving to do our best with what we have been given, we are making an effort to achieve for the glory of God; and, as a result, will receive the crown that will last forever.

FATHER, IT IS SO EASY FOR US TO TAKE ALL THE CREDIT FOR OUR ACCOMPLISHMENTS. WE KNOW YOU HAVE GIVEN US ALL KINDS OF EXAMPLES IN YOUR WORD ABOUT WHAT HAPPENS TO PEOPLE WHEN THEY DO THIS. YET, WE STILL DO IT. FATHER, HELP US TO PRAISE YOU WHEN WE HAVE SUCCESS AND HELP US REALIZE THAT IT IS BECAUSE OF YOUR GRACE THAT WE ARE ABLE TO DO ALL THINGS. HELP US TO GET OUR PRIORITIES STRAIGHT AND TO MAKE AN EFFORT TO SEEK YOUR PRAISE RATHER THAN MAN'S PRAISE. AMEN

CHAPTER 12

Pride in Knowledge

In previous chapters we briefly alluded to the problem many people have controlling their pride in, what they consider to be, their "superior" knowledge. It seems, for many of us, our problems with pride are proportional to how knowledgeable we believe we are! Have you ever observed someone who has acquired quite a bit of education in their field; and, because of their "higher education", give the impression that they are superior? We see this in all occupations—educators, scientists, lawyers, doctors; and, even, occasionally, with preachers of the Word! When a person spends six to ten years studying in institutions of higher learning, they are bound to gain some knowledge. At least, they usually know much more about their field than those who have not had this time of formal study. Because they have become knowledgeable in a particular field, they often are considered to be "experts" in their respective fields and become sought after by groups throughout their local, national, and international communities. As a result, people can very easily become "puffed up" with pride because of the accumulated knowledge, respect, fame, and, often, fortune, they attain. An age-old axiom defines an educated person as ONE WHO KNOWS HOW LITTLE HE KNOWS!

People with an above average education, who subscribe to this philosophy, cannot very easily get too serious about what they know, because they can't help but realize how much there is that they do NOT know. This realization helps to keep pride under control.

As Christians, we cannot escape the fact that throughout the Bible we are taught that there is a knowledge that comes from man, and there is a knowledge that is from God. Knowledge is simply an acquaintance with facts, truths, or principles. Man, using his intellect, has developed a body of knowledge in every field of endeavor. Through the scientific method (which, by the way, is only one way of obtaining the truth), man has developed a great amount of knowledge. Man, as a result of the acquisition of such a great quantity of knowledge at this point in time, has come to the belief, according to secular humanism, that he (man), with his great knowledge and capability to acquire knowledge, can solve any and all of the problems of mankind. Where does this leave God and the knowledge he reveals to us through His Word? The Christian does not have to go into God's Word very far to see what God has to say about all of this. In the very first book of the Bible, Genesis, the second chapter, God clearly tells us there are two kinds of knowledge: "In the middle of the garden were the tree of life and the tree of the knowledge of good and evil". (Genesis 2:9) Not only are we told that there is good knowledge and that there is evil knowledge, we are also told that Adam had a moral choice to make. He was commanded not to eat from the tree of the knowledge of good and evil, for if he did he would also have evil knowledge! He already had knowledge of "good". All that he had already seen and experienced was good. By refusing to obey God's command to not eat of the tree of knowledge of good and evil, Adam chose to have the knowledge of evil!

We can easily look at Adam and say "what a weak character he was"! He had it made and he blew it! But, are we really any different from Adam? Today, every one of us has a similar choice to make. We can accept God's knowledge as supreme, or we can reject God's knowledge and accept man's. But you say, "Can't some of man's knowledge be good? After all, God gave us the intellect to learn and know things! He gave us physical laws in science upon which we govern our physical world! Is all of man's knowledge evil?" The answer, of course, is NO, as long as man's knowledge does not conflict with God's knowledge. There are many, many examples that could be given to illustrate this point. Let's look at the field of archaeology. Man's knowledge takes this view. If, with our modern science, we come across an archaeological find that gives credence to what the Bible says, then we say that science is proving the Bible to be true (at least a little bit of it!). That logic is backward to the believer who believes that God's Word is infallible. If we reverse the logic, we would come to the conclusion that the archaeological find was accurate because it is substantiated by the Bible. With God's knowledge, the Bible is the "baseline" for truth rather than modern day "science". This reasoning can be applied to all phases of thinking from quantum physics to psychology and sociology. Through Solomon, God gave us the teaching: "The fear of the Lord is the beginning of knowledge, but fools despise wisdom and discipline." (Proverbs 1:7) We all have to make a choice to accept God's knowledge or man's. The human being who chooses to deny the very existence of God is not going to use His Word as a "baseline" for anything!

New Testament writers were well aware of the problem of men becoming reliant on man's knowledge. Paul was trying to explain to converted pagans the difference regarding their knowledge about eating food that has been sacrificed to idols and the assurance that God "knows them": "Now about food sacrificed to idols: We know that we all possess knowledge. Knowledge puffs up, but love builds up. The man who thinks he knows something does not yet know as he ought to know. But the man who loves God is known by God." (1 Corinthians 8:1-3) Paul was saying that EVERYONE KNOWS about the custom of food being sacrificed to idols, but EXPERIENCING THE LOVE OF GOD (being known by God) is foreign to some men. In Paul's first letter to Timothy he reminds him to: ". . .guard what has been entrusted to your care. Turn away from godless chatter and the opposing ideas of what is falsely called knowledge, which some have professed and in so doing have wandered from the faith." (1 Timothy 6:20-21) Apparently, it was as easy then as it is today to be misled about whose (man's or God's) knowledge is supreme.

The writer of Romans describes how the wrath of God falls on mankind when His knowledge is rejected. "Furthermore, since they did not think it worthwhile to retain the knowledge of God he gave them over to a depraved mind to do what ought not to be done. They have become filled with every kind of wickedness, evil, greed and depravity. They are full of envy, murder, strife, deceit and malice. They are gossips, slanderers, God-haters, insolent, arrogant and boastful; . . ." (Romans 1:28-30) Does this sound like man today? One might say that it almost sounds like a summary of TODAY'S newspaper! Jude also described conceited Godless men when he was describing the day of judgment: "These men are grumblers and fault-finders; they follow their own evil desires; they boast about themselves and flatter others for their own advantage." (Jude, verse 16) Here Jude seems to be describing the secular humanists throughout all time who have rejected God and promoted their own hedonistic values.

Jesus Christ really blasted the law of His day, and His words are also relevant today. He said: "Woe to you experts in the law, because you have taken away the key to knowledge.

"Who is wise and understanding among you? Let him show
it by his good life, by deeds done in the humility
that comes from wisdom."
James 3:13

You yourselves have not entered, and you have hindered those who were entering." (Luke 11:52) Wow! Does that ever speak to our world as it exists today! Many of our laws and nearly all of the new laws being written today ignore God's knowledge! Can you imagine what God thinks about laws which legalize the killing of unborn babies; laws denying nourishment to newborn babies because they have a defect; making doctors legally responsible for informing parents that their child may be born with a defect just so they might have the opportunity to abort the child?

In Genesis we get a glimpse of what it must have been like when Adam knew only good. Before the fall, Adam was full of God's knowledge and was in close communion with God. To completely grasp this relationship is difficult for us today, but we are given many little clues about what it would be like, and is like, when we are "right with God". We know that our love of Christ surpasses any knowledge that we may obtain on earth (Ephesians 3:19). "For God, who said, 'Let light shine out of darkness,' made His light of the knowledge of the glory of God in the face of Christ." (2 Corinthians 4:6) We also know that we are to grow in the grace and knowledge of our Lord and Savior Jesus Christ (2 Peter 3:18). As Christians, then, we know that true knowledge is the knowledge of Jesus Christ and His will! Paul was trying to get this point across to the brothers in Colosse when he said: "For this reason, since the day we heard about you, we have not stopped praying for you and asking God to fill you with the knowledge of his will through all spiritual wisdom and understanding." (Colossians 1:9) How great it would be today if all Christians would constantly pray for the leaders of our country to have spiritual wisdom and understanding of God's knowledge! It's going to happen! We know that in the future, the earth will be full of the knowledge of the Lord. (Isaiah 11:9)

WE KNOW there is a difference between man's knowledge and God's knowledge, and we also KNOW that God's knowledge is eternal and man's knowledge will pass away. We need to constantly keep this in mind when we establish our priorities and distribute our time and effort between increasing our knowledge of earthly things and God's knowledge.

A word closely related to knowledge is wisdom. Generally, wisdom is defined as the "right use of knowledge". Knowledge can be used for good or evil. One who has wisdom would use his/her knowledge for good. One who has wisdom would make good use of their knowledge. One could still argue the point, however, that wisdom may be relative to what one regards as good. The wise old bank robber or embezzler may make "good use of his knowledge" and not be caught, but the Christian would insist that is not the "right" use of knowledge and, therefore, is an unwise act. Therefore, the whole idea of wisdom comes down to what one regards as "good" or "right". The secular humanist believes that since everything is relative and everyone should have the right to do what pleases them, what is "good" and "right" is up to the individual. So, technically, there could be a wise secular humanist. The Christian, on the other hand, has a standard of "good" and "right" established by his Creator and revealed to us through his Son and His Holy Word. If one were to have perfect wisdom, one would have to have perfect knowledge, and only the infinite Creator has that perfection. That all knowing, all wise Creator God is our "baseline" for what is good and right.

Paul clearly teaches us what the source of our wisdom is in his first letter to the Corinthians. "Where is the wise man? Where is the scholar? Where is the philosopher of this age? Has not God made foolish the wisdom of the world? For since in the wisdom of God the world through its wisdom did not know him, God was pleased through the foolishness of what was preached to save those who believe. Jews demand miraculous signs and Greeks look for wisdom, but we preach Christ crucified: a stumbling block to Jews and foolishness to Gentiles, but to those whom God has called, both Jews and Greeks, Christ the power of God and the wisdom of God". (1 Corinthians 1:20-24) We can ask the same question today that Paul asked the Corinthians. Where are the wise men? Where are the scholars? Where is the philosopher of our age? Is there really any secular humanist that is making the world better today? We have to agree with Paul that even today God has indeed made foolish the wisdom of the world. Paul continues with his teaching on this point in verse 30. "It is because of him that you are in Jesus Christ, who has become for us wisdom from God-that is, our righteousness, holiness and redemption." All wisdom is embodied in Jesus Christ. We need no other model. We only need to look to Christ and his teachings to know what God's wisdom is.

Paul also shows us how God reveals his wisdom through the Holy Spirit. "My message and my preaching were not with wise and persuasive words, but with a demonstration of the Spirit's power, so that your faith might not rest on men's wisdom, but on God's power. We do, however, speak a message of wisdom among the mature, but not the wisdom of this age or of the rulers of this age, who are coming to nothing. No, we speak of God's secret wisdom, a wisdom that has been hidden and that God destined for our glory before time began". (1 Corinthians 2:4-7) We are commanded not to rely on man's wisdom. It is folly, capricious, and comes to nothing. What is of lasting value is God's wisdom that we receive from the life of Jesus Christ, his teaching, and from the leading of the Holy Spirit. "Although they claimed to be wise, they became fools" (Romans 1:22) pretty well sums up God's view of man's wisdom.

So far we have briefly examined knowledge and wisdom from both man's view and God's view. We began the discussion by indicating that it seems that the more knowledge we have, the more susceptible we are to becoming prideful. One might think that when man adds "goodness" to an abundance of knowledge he would not be susceptible to pride! In the introduction to this book it was mentioned that a famous architect once said that early in life he had to choose between "honest arrogance" and "hypocritical humility" and he chose honest arrogance and found no reason to change. This is typical of MAN! Why was it necessary to have to be one or the other? He could also have chosen to give God credit for his special ability and become a truly honest AND humble person. James summarizes this idea in describing the two kinds of wisdom. "Who is wise and understanding among you? Let him show it by his good life, by deeds done in the humility that comes from wisdom." (James 3:13) James goes on to explain that the "other wisdom" is earthly and from Satan.

What then is our duty as Christians? If we believe we have a great deal of knowledge EITHER of a secular or spiritual nature, we must show sincere wisdom by relating that knowledge to God's righteousness and goodness, and thereby give Him the credit. This is our duty and, if we do this, we cannot help being truly humble. If we humble ourselves under God's mighty hand we will be lifted up in due time, that is, in God's time. (1 Peter 5:6 paraphrased) Also, in Proverbs 15:33, we read: "The fear of the Lord teaches a man wisdom, and humility comes before honor." As a result of our humility, God honors us in His time! We will be held accountable at the day of judgment for our arrogance, or honored for our humility. Micah summarizes many of these points in one small but powerful teaching: "He has showed you, O man, what is good. And what does the Lord require of you? To act justly and to love mercy and to walk humbly with your God". (Micah 6:8)

Isaiah, in his prophecy regarding Babylon, really sums

up the attitude of our society today. "You have trusted in your wickedness and have said, "No one sees me." Your wisdom and knowledge mislead you when you say to yourself, "I am, and there is no one besides me." (Isaiah 47:10) What a description of secular humanism! With all of man's knowledge and wisdom today we still seem to insist that the "I am, and there is none besides me" attitude is sufficient to meet all our needs! If this is a true premise, why is the world in such a mess? Why has not man learned with all his knowledge and wisdom that he CANNOT make men righteous! Satan knows the answer to this question and, as the father of pride, delights in seeing men refuse to acknowledge their creator by giving Him credit. Satan wants men to worship anything other than the true living God.

The prophet Zephaniah warns us to: "Seek the Lord, all you humble of the land, you who do what he commands, seek righteousness, seek humility." (Zephaniah 2:3) This is our duty, to praise God for any knowledge and wisdom we have been given, and to seek humility. To seek means to try to attain. That rather implies that humility is not easy or "natural" for man. Rather, we have to work at becoming humble by continually remembering from whence all our knowledge, wisdom, and ability come.

FATHER IN HEAVEN, THIS IS A TOUGH LESSON FOR MANY TO LEARN. KNOWLEDGE IS VALUED IN OUR SOCIETY SO MUCH. WE OFTEN ARE CONCEITED BECAUSE OF WHAT WE KNOW. NOT ONLY DO WE BECOME CONCEITED, BUT WE ENJOY BEING WISE–OR BELIEVING WE ARE WISE. FATHER, HELP US TO REMEMBER WHAT THE SOURCE OF PRIDE IS AND WHY SATAN WANTS US TO TAKE PRIDE IN OUR KNOWLEDGE AND WISDOM. WE KNOW, LORD, THAT HE IS TRYING DESPERATELY TO SEPARATE US FROM YOU. LORD, WE

ASK FOR YOUR PROTECTION FROM THE INFLU-ENCE OF SATAN RELATING TO PRIDE IN OUR KNOWLEDGE. HELP US TO RECOGNIZE THAT TRUE KNOWLEDGE AND WISDOM COME FROM YOU THROUGH YOUR SON JESUS CHRIST AND THROUGH YOUR HOLY SPIRIT. WE THANK YOU FOR THOSE GIFTS, THAT WE KNOW WHAT OUR SOURCE IS, AND THAT WE ARE NOT DEPENDENT ON MANKIND FOR TRUTH. IN JESUS'NAME WE PRAY. AMEN.

CHAPTER 13

Spiritual Pride

In previous chapters we have seen how Satan works hard on Christians. He does not need to spend much time hassling non-Christians because they are already "his". Because Satan is at war with God, his primary target is the Christian; and he wants to enlist as many mortals as he can for the battles. One area where Satan really attacks us is through our spiritual pride. If Satan can cause spiritual people to be proud people, he has taken a great stride forward in his war. "Spiritual" people (i.e., God's people who are attempting to spread the Gospel to all people) are usually looked upon as being holy. Being a holy person means that one is set apart from the values and customs of the world and follows God's laws. If Satan can get these holy people to fall into the sin of pride, he has a real weapon to use to show how hypocritical Christians are! Unfortunately, there are many "Elmer Gantry types" in the world. Their prideful lust for power has led them astray, and they become examples (hypocritical Christians) for non-Christians to use against Christianity.

When we were discussing the concept of pride in accomplishments, we briefly mentioned the one who is highly successful in preaching the Gospel. We also noted that often pride is proportional to the success one has in any field of endeavor. It must be very difficult for a personality who is highly respected as a man of God throughout the world to remain humble. Knowing that hundreds of thousands of people are watching you in person, or on television, listening to your message of salvation, and that many of these people will make a decision for Christ that will affect their eternal life, places a tremendous amount of responsibility on the evangelist to remain humble. Through media techniques available to us today, we have the opportunity to preach the Gospel to many times the number of people the apostles could reach. We need to pray often for humility for those ministers who are using the media to spread the Gospel of Jesus Christ. We need to pray that they will remain honest and humble as they develop the large organizations necessary for worldwide evangelical work and pray that they remember it is Jesus Christ who is to be glorified through their ministry—not themselves. They are indeed human vessels and, therefore, subject to the sin of pride.

Satan also loves to work on theologians. Have you ever wondered why so many people go to seminary as Christians and come out as academicians? With man's way of obtaining knowledge, the seminary student is taught to critically evaluate every word of scripture and to develop large research papers on theological doctrines such as predestination, tribulation, grace, and the like. It is very easy, in this environment of theological study, to become so "academic" and prideful of one's new found knowledge about Christianity to stray from the faith they once had. Do not misunderstand. The Christian scholar should be a competent student of the Gospel. The point here is that academic study in itself often leads one to become spiritually prideful. Knowing a lot about theology, being a Biblical scholar, being an expert in prophecy, knowing church history well, or specializing in Biblical numerology, does not lead one to salvation in and of itself.

Peter, in his second letter, spends the whole second chapter talking about false teachers and their fate. One of the traits of these false teachers is their pride. They may have once even believed the truth; but because of the power they obtained, they became prideful and began mouthing empty, boastful words and told the people what they wanted to hear instead of what the Word says. "They promise them freedom, while they themselves are slaves of depravity-for a man is a slave to whatever has mastered him." (2 Peter 2:19) Once spiritual pride is established it can dominate a man and lead to his destruction. Even a pastor of a local congregation is not exempt from the possibility of falling into the sin of pride.

We also see the problem of pride entering into the leadership of the church body. In Paul's first letter to Timothy he was telling him about the qualifications of leaders in the fellowship and reminded him that those appointed should not be recent converts lest they become conceited and fall under the same judgment as the devil. (1 Timothy 3:6) If this is a potential problem for those who are lay leaders in the body, think of what a potential problem it must be for preachers and evangelists. And, also, look at what Paul said was the result-they will fall under the same judgment as the Devil! Obviously, spiritual pride was a potential problem for early church leaders just as it is for leaders today. That really should not be a surprise to us; for we, as Christians, should realize that "human nature" has not changed since the days of Adam and Eve!

Now, here is where we as lay people can get smug and say "those church leaders really have to be careful of becoming prideful"; and, by doing so, assume that it is not a problem for us! Sorry, that's just not true! Have you ever seen a lay person, in his intense desire to serve the Lord, witness in such a boisterous manner that it appears as though he is trying to show the world how spiritual he is? Christians

"for they loved praise from men more
than praise from God."
John 12:43

often feel a need to demonstrate how spiritual they are by expressing to others their "good deeds", their success at evangelizing, their knowledge of a certain doctrine, showing others how worn their old Bible is, and so on. Unfortunately, they are often more interested in receiving praise from their Christian peers than they are in receiving praise from God. This also is a human trait that has been around for a long time, and we have to be constantly aware that it exists and make an effort at avoiding falling into that trap. Jesus, in his testimony as to who he was, said: "How can you believe if you accept praise from one another, yet make no effort to obtain the praise that comes from the only God?" (John 5:44) Realizing that the praise we should seek comes from God and not man is a hard lesson to learn. We should conduct our lives in a humble manner at all times. God knows what we are doing for Him-we don't have to tell Him, or anyone else!

Sinful conduct can easily creep into a body of believers and; if not checked, can gradually become the norm. This was true in the early church, and it is true today. There are many examples in the scriptures that describe these situations. Today, some are more subtle, but just as serious. When Paul wrote the Corinthians about judging the conduct of believers, he referred directly to the problem of boasting and how it can spread. "Your boasting is not good. Don't you know that a little yeast works through the whole batch of dough?" (1 Corinthians 5:6) If we associate with a group of Christians who accept boasting about their accomplishments as the "in thing" to do, it can soon become the norm for the group! We are to serve the Lord with great humility and need to remind one another of this truth from time to time.

The fact that some people fall into the sin of pride should not surprise us. Paul reminded Timothy that in the last days there would be rampant Godlessness, that people would be lovers of themselves, lovers of money, they would be boastful, proud, conceited, and so on. And what are we to do about these believers? Certainly we should attempt to help them with their pride problem, pray for them; and, if this does not help, have nothing to do with them! (2 Timothy 3:1-5)

The results of being a proud Christian are clearly stated in the Bible. We can be isolated or alienated from other believers and/or fall under the same judgment as the Devil! Spiritual pride is a serious sin in God's eyes. The more responsibility we have in the body of believers, the more we have to fight the temptation of spiritual pride, and the more we have to work at being humble. What, then, should we do? How do we prevent ourselves from developing spiritual pride? The apostle Peter gives us a great exhortation on making our calling sure in the first chapter of his second epistle.

This second letter of Peter's was written to the body of the church to warn them of the false teachers that were creeping into fellowships. These false teachers were called "antinomians", and were men who used God's grace as justification for sinning. They practiced just about every sin imaginable and justified their conduct, based on the premise man is imperfect and he is bound to sin; and, since he is covered by the grace of God, in spite of his carnal nature, he is justified in sinning! This whole concept is rooted in self-gratification, which is inseparable from pride. Specifically, these false teachers were bold, arrogant, and boastful. (2 Peter 2:10, 18) Peter proceeds to teach us what we should be doing to prevent falling into the same trap.

Peter begins the first chapter by telling us about all that God has done for us; followed by what we should do, in return, for God. Peter begins his "case" by explaining what being a bondservant means. If we choose to follow Christ as our master, then we are committed to GROW in our faith. Peter tells us how God has given us EVERYTHING we need to live our lives-not some things, but everything we need. Throughout the Bible we have seen repeated teachings about how humility is a virtue and pride is a sin. We have the KNOWLEDGE, but how do we keep from falling into these sins? Verse 5 of chapter 1 is the key to the point Peter was trying to make: ". . . make every effort to . . .". Make an effort to do what? To GROW! Faith in Jesus Christ is our foundation as Christians—the basic essential upon which all Christians grow. Have you ever seen a Christian who made a commitment to Christ many years ago, but is still in the "milk" stage of spiritual growth? These are the Christians who are often "siphoned off" by religious sects. They have made a decision for Christ, but have grown so little that they can be deceived and led astray very easily by false teachers. Peter was teaching that the Christian life should not be an initial spasm followed by resting inertia.

Peter makes a very strong, logical case here for us. Because of our relationship to a God, with all His infinite powers and wisdom, who has given us everything we need for life, we should make every effort to grow in our faith. This gift is so great it should not be taken for granted-we should desire to know more of Him upon whom we have placed our faith. Peter then lists seven areas on which we should grow and build our faith. The first thing to add to our faith is goodness. This means moral excellence, uprightness, virtue, and courage. Secondly, we should add knowledge. Not man's knowledge, but God's knowledge! To knowledge we are to add self-control. This means taking a good grip on ourselves, being in control of our lives, and living tempered lives. We have complete control of how much time we are going to spend each day in prayer and the study of God's word-right? To self-control we should add perseverance. This is steadfastness in enduring the daily trials that all of us have to face in the world-it is "keeping the faith" in spite of all the bad things we come face to face with each day. To perseverance we should add Godliness. In the Greek this has a twofold meaning. It means that we should work at increasing our relationship with our creator God, and it also means, because of this man-God relationship, we must work at improving our relationship with our fellow man. Godliness here has both the vertical and horizontal relationship. To Godliness we are to add brotherly kindness. This is the "Philadelphia" brotherliness, or the love of brothers and sisters "in the Lord". And finally, lest we feel we only have a responsibility to love other Christians, Peter tells us to add to brotherly kindness, love. This love is love for all people outside the church.

Next, Peter points out the fact that we have a CHOICE. We can chose to remain "milk Christians", or we can choose to GROW. If we choose not to grow in these seven areas, we will be ineffective in our knowledge of our Lord, we will be unproductive, we will be nearsighted, we will be blind, and we will be forgetful of the greatness of our salvation. WOW! What a conviction! Have you ever felt that you may be a rather "ineffective" Christian? Have you ever felt that you are not growing, not bringing others to Christ, or cannot defend your faith? When we do get this feeling, we should look to 1 Peter and examine the efforts we are making to grow in our faith!

If this has sounded a bit negative thus far, we now come to the good part. Peter tells us what will happen to us if we DO make an effort to GROW. Peter says: "For if you do these things, you will never fall, and you will receive a rich welcome into the eternal kingdom of our Lord and Savior Jesus Christ." (2 Peter 1:10) What a confidence builder! If we do these things we will NEVER FALL! We fall away from God when we look to the world for solutions. If we do these seven things, we will be looking to God; and we will find EVERY-THING we need for life, and WE WILL never fall!

It is difficult to see, after examining Peter's teaching here, how we could possibly fall into the sin of pride, IF we are growing in these seven areas. God's grace is indeed sufficient for us; and, as we make an effort to come into a closer relationship with Christ by learning His will, it will be very difficult to become prideful people. "Let us grow near to God with a sincere heart in full assurance of faith. . . ." (Hebrews 10:22) As we grow nearer to God, we automatically become more humble. To know the greatness of God cannot help but make us humble. To grow near to God with a sincere heart, gives us the power to be free from spiritual pride, regardless of our station in life; that is, whether we are a great evangelist, a preacher, a teacher, or a "lay" servant of God.

GOD IN HEAVEN, WE PRAY THAT YOU WILL KEEP US FROM BEING SPIRITUALLY SMUG. TOO OFTEN WE SEEK THE PRAISE OF MAN AND TEND TO BOAST OF OUR SPIRITUAL ACCOMPLISHMENTS. WE KNOW, FATHER, THAT IF WE ARE REALLY MAKING AN EFFORT TO GROW IN OUR KNOWLEDGE OF YOU, IT WILL BE IMPOSSIBLE TO BE PRIDEFUL. BY KNOWING YOUR GREATNESS AND YOUR TEACHING ON PRIDE IN OUR LIVES, WE CAN AVOID THIS TEMPTATION TO WANT TO TAKE CREDIT FOR OUR OWN "SPIRITUAL" GROWTH AND ACCOMPLISHMENTS. WE KNOW, FATHER, THAT YOU ARE INDEED THE SOURCE FROM WHICH ALL THINGS WE HAVE COME; AND ASK THAT YOU PROTECT US FROM THE SIN OF BEING SPIRITUALLY PROUD, BECAUSE WE KNOW IT BECOMES A STUMBLING BLOCK TO OTHERS IN THEIR WALK AND CAN EVEN BECOME AN OBSTACLE TO SOME ACCEPTING YOU AS THEIR SAVIOR. IN JESUS' NAME WE PRAY. AMEN.

CHAPTER 14

Pride in Good Works

Very often we encounter dear people who have a great spirit when it comes to giving and serving. The gift God has given them is that of serving, and they use their gift in an efficient and humble manner. They often stay "behind the scenes" and do not even get recognition for their good works. In fact, very often they are unknown to the persons they are helping! They desire to help others because of their love for God and their praise comes from God rather than from man. These people are not only pleasing God by using their gift, but they are tremendous examples for others of us who have not been blessed with this gift.

More frequently throughout history, man has been more interested in doing good works so that he may be "glorified" and praised by his peers! Even the Sadducees and Pharisees had this problem during the time of Christ, and Christ used that as an example of what man ought not do. He told the people and his disciples not to mimic them because they were hypocrites. "Everything they do is done for men to see; they make their phylacteries (little boxes in which their scripture verses were carried) wide and the tassels on their garments long; they love the place of honor at banquets and the most important seats in the synagogues; they love to be greeted in the marketplaces and to have men call them Rabbi." (Matthew 23:5-7) "Everything they do is done for men to see" summarizes man's motive for good works throughout most of history! Man basically wants to look good to others, and he will often do unbelievable things to show his peers how "good" he is. Man's way is to please his fellow man with good works, thus, building his own ego rather than serving to please God and receive His praise.

Many Jews, before the time of Christ, held that merit could be stored up by meticulously observing the law. These Jews believed that observing the law, regardless of how "mechanical", was the way to salvation. The Jew believed, because judgment was in the future and it was based upon works, one could never do enough "works", for you never knew whether you had done enough to make salvation before death. This is also true today for some religions. That their lives were already justified as a result of the work of Christ was a difficult concept for Paul to get across to the Jews who had become converted to Christianity. The verdict of "guilty but pardoned", rather than "guilty and condemned" had already been declared. Earlier Isaiah relayed to the Jews God's accusation against the wicked when he said: "I will expose your righteousness and your works, and they will not benefit you." (Isaiah 57:12) The Jews knew better, and we know better today, yet we still take great pride in our good works! God knows whether we are doing good works to please Him, or to feed our own pride and show others how good we are.

In Chapters 3 and 4 of the Book of Romans, Paul goes into great depth to explain this concept. Verse 27 (Chapter 3) sums up most of the teaching in relation to the concept of pride: "Where, then, is boasting? It is excluded. On what principle? On that of observing the law? No, but on that of faith." Righteousness comes through faith, not by works. Paul further explains this in his writing to the Ephesians

"For it is by grace you have been saved, through faith—and this is not from yourselves, it is the gift of God—not by works, so that no one can boast."
Ephesians 2:8-9

through a well known and often quoted verse: "For It Is by grace you have been saved, through faith-and this not from yourselves, it is the gift of God-not by works, so that no one can boast." (Ephesians 2:8-9) If it were possible for us to gain salvation through works, then Christians would be very busy gaining "brownie points" as fast as they could in order to gain salvation through their own efforts, therefore, claiming "I did it! I earned enough good works points to assure my salvation!" Sorry, it just doesn't work that way!

Sometimes when people study this topic they refer to the writings of James. James states that: ". . . faith by itself, if it is not accompanied by action, is dead." (James 2:17) James and Paul were really not teaching two different things. James was not thinking of works in the sense of legal works, rather, works in the sense of benevolence, or a recognition of the social implications of the Gospel. Another way of expressing what James was teaching is that WORKS FLOW NATURALLY FROM FAITH! Our faith is made complete as a result of our actions. In other words, a man is justified in his claim to have faith if his works demonstrate the reality of his claim. Can you see the difference here between doing good works to glorify God because of our faith, compared to doing good works in a legal sense?

Wise Solomon gave us a proverb related to this subject. "Like clouds and wind without rain is a man who boasts of gifts he does not give". (Proverbs 25:14) If we boast about our gift of giving or serving, believing it is a legalistic thing we must do, rather than using this gift given to us by God to serve others as an expression of our heart, we are like clouds and wind without any substance. Jesus said: "He who speaks on his own does so to gain honor for himself, but he who works for the honor of the one who sent him is a man of truth; there is nothing false about him." (John 7:18) There it is right from our Lord! Those who are doing good works because of their own pride are false, that is, their motive is wrong.

When we compare our works with that of the Lord we cannot help but be humbled. The Bible is full of descriptions of what the Lord has done. "Great are the works of the Lord; they are pondered by all who delight in them". (Psalm 11:2) "Praise the Lord, all his works everywhere in his dominion". (Psalm 103:22) We could go on and on examining scriptures that show the great works of Christ. If we ponder on how great the works of Christ are, we can't possibly help but realize how minor our contribution is, nor would we desire to boast about them. If our works are done for the honor of the one who created all, for the one who gave us everything we need for life, and if those works are a result of our faith, then we are truly honoring God and not trying to build ourselves up. "Those who have served well gain an excellent standing and great assurance in their faith in Christ Jesus." (1 Timothy 3:13)

Peter teaches us how we should live together in harmony and humility. "Finally, all of you, live in harmony with one another; be sympathetic, love as brothers, be compassionate and humble." (1 Peter 3:8) So as we live together, we should serve one another in gladness that we are doing what pleases God. We should not serve one another simply because it will look good for us in the eyes of others. When we do good works because of our own pride we are not living the truth, rather we are living a false life that glorifies self, and therefore, Satan!

When we see a brother or sister in need we shouldn't ask them what we can do for them. Have you ever said to anyone-if there is anything I can do for you, don't hesitate to call me! That's the wrong way! What we are really saying is that we will help them-IF they ask us! If people are really in need, why should they have to ask? Many people are simply too inhibited or self-reliant to ask, feeling that they do not want to impose on others! We should be sensitive enough, as Christians living out our faith, to find out what their needs are and fulfill those needs by doing what has to be done without asking; and, even without the benefactor of the good deed knowing who did it! That's God's way! It may not seem to be a "self-fulfilling" deed, but whom are we trying to please— ourselves, Satan, or God?

FATHER, THIS IDEA OF TAKING PRIDE IN THE WORKS WE DO IS A REAL PROBLEM FOR MOST OF US. IT IS SO INGRAINED IN US BECAUSE OF OUR UPBRINGING THAT WE FEEL WE MUST SHOW OTHERS THE GOOD DEEDS WE DO. WE CAN'T HELP BUT ACKNOWLEDGE THAT WE ARE BUILDING OUR OWN EGO WHEN WE DO THIS, YET WE STILL HAVE A GREAT FEELING OF PRIDE WHEN WE DO A GOOD DEED. FATHER, HELP US TO DEVELOP A SPIRIT OF SERVING AND HELPING OTHERS SO THAT WE WANT TO DO THIS BECAUSE OF OUR LOVE FOR YOU. BECAUSE YOU FIRST LOVED US AND HAVE GIVEN US EVERYTHING WE NEED FOR LIFE, HELP US TO HAVE GIVING SPIRITS. HELP US TO GLORIFY YOU IN A LOVING WAY THROUGH OUR DEEDS. IN JESUS' NAME. AMEN.

CHAPTER 15

Pride in Military Might

Not long ago there was great controversy over whether we need to build up the defenses of our country. Since September 11, 2001, things have changed drastically. Now the controversy is not should we, but how much should we build up our defenses and in what way! Every day our news sources are saturated with the war on terror, the politics involved, asking who are our real allies in this battle, how is the country going to finance this new challenge, and how we can use our military capabilities most effectively. Pride in our nation and its military has come to the forefront. When we refer here to pride in our military might, are we are not talking about those men and women who, without even a second thought, put their lives on the line to preserve the freedoms this country holds so dear; rather, we are referring to our position as the strongest nation in the world.

The specific problem we are dealing with in this book, pride, is probably the fundamental problem involved in the defense buildup issue. Before September 11, we might have asked, are we genuinely concerned about the welfare of our country and the perpetuation of our way of life in justifying a defense buildup, or are we simply desirous of becoming the greatest country in the world because we are a proud people?

The issue at first glance may seem simple, but gathering data to really be convinced of the truth, is not so simple. Who do you believe-the liberals, the conservatives, foreign governments, our government, Christians or non-Christians? If we could gather data from a variety of sources—liberals, conservatives, foreign governments, our government, Christians, non-Christians, synthesize all the facts, and come to the conclusion that increasing our national defense was necessary for the survival of our freedom, we could be justified in supporting a defense buildup. However, if after analyzing all the facts, we were to find we are in the position of being the greatest nation on earth and are invincible because of our strength, we could become very proud of our national strength and want to keep increasing it in order to maintain our national esteem throughout the world. It is difficult, if not impossible, however, for a proud country to see its own faults. If we were indeed one nation under God, it would be very difficult to keep from being a justifiably proud country. BUT, even though our founding fathers declared us to be a nation under God, today it is questionable, yet we are a proud country!

Pride in military might can probably be best seen by examining national defense installations, defense training facilities, defense weaponry and personnel. If an individual were to have a guided tour of submarine bases, air bases, defense centers, fly in the latest military jets, tour the great battleships, and tour research facilities where work was being done on weapons of war, they could not escape a sense of awe and be rather proud of our defense capabilities.

When we begin to believe that we can live without God in a secular humanistic society, can build the greatest weapons of destruction, and can control our own destiny, we can easily become a very proud nation. We know this to be a fact because we have seen numerous examples in secular and Biblical writings where this has been the case.

Isaiah was giving his people this message from God in the following prophesy: "Woe to those who go down to Egypt for help, who rely on horses, who trust in the multitude of their chariots and in the great strength of their horsemen, but do not look to the Holy One of Israel, or seek help from the Lord." (Isaiah 31:1) God was explaining (through Isaiah) a problem that has been common to man throughout history. If you put your trust, confidence, and hope in your great strength, as measured by your military might, rather than seeking help from God, you are destined to fail. On many occasions, during Old Testament times, armies who were greatly undermanned and had fewer war machines than their opponents, won wars because God was with them and the people relied on HIM!

Daniel tells us of the battles between the kings of the south and the north in Daniel Chapter 11. "When the army is carried off, the king of the south will be filled with pride and will slaughter many thousands, yet will not remain triumphant." (Daniel 11:12) The king of the south became so proud of his conquests, power, and military might that he fell into that Satanic trap of thinking "who needs God?"—I have such great power and have had such great military success—I am god! He became so proud that his reign was very short lived. This also rings true today. We have become such a great nation, and now have become a society that does not feel a need for reliance on God, that one must ponder as to how long we can last as a great nation!

In Chapter two of Deuteronomy, Moses also gives us a good example of this same problem. After wandering in the desert for a long time, the Israelites were told by God to cross the Jordan and go forth and conquer the Amorites. But before they attacked they decided it might be in their best interest to send spies ahead to see what was in store for them, even though God had told them to do it and that He would be with them! The spies returned with word that the

"Woe to those who go down to Egypt for help,
who rely on horses, who trust in the multitude of their
chariots and in the great strength of their horsemen,
but do not look to the Holy One of Israel,
or seek help from the Lord."
Isaiah 31:1

Amorite cities were large, had walls up to the sky, and that the people were stronger and taller than they were. So they became frightened and did not do as the Lord commanded. Then after Moses explained to them what they had done and the consequences thereof, they changed their minds and decided that maybe it would be better, after all, if they did go ahead and try to conquer the Amorites. Moses told them: "But the Lord said to me, 'Tell them, Do not go up and fight, because I will not be with you. You will be defeated by your enemies', so I told you, but you would not listen. You rebelled against the Lord's command and in your arrogance you marched up into the hill country. The Amorites who lived in those hills came out against you; they chased you like a swarm of bees and beat you down from Seir all the way to Hormah. You came back and wept before the Lord, but he paid no attention to your weeping and turned a deaf ear to you." (Deuteronomy 1:42-45) They were not only defeated in battle, but forced to return to the desert around the hill country of Seir, all a result of distrusting God and not following his commands. In man's way of thinking, we assess our capabilities then make a decision based on our assessment and act without seeking God's will!

This whole issue of putting our trust in our military might or in God is summarized by King David. "From heaven the Lord looks down and sees all mankind; from his dwelling place he watches all who live on earth-he who forms the hearts of all, who considers everything they do. No king is saved by the size of his army; no warrior escapes by his great strength. A horse is a vain hope for deliverance; despite all its great strength it cannot save. But the eyes of the Lord are on those who fear him, on those whose hope is in his unfailing love, to deliver them from death and keep them alive in famine." (Psalm 33:13-19) All we have to do to change this Psalm and make it relevant to today is change "horse" to: jet fighter, missile, ship, tank, and so on. Great military weapons, regardless of whether they are horses or tanks CANNOT SAVE MAN! All Christians, regardless of their stance on the defense of their nation must learn from the Word of God that military might, in and of itself, cannot save mankind or nations. Man without God is not only helpless, but destined to fall!

The examples stated here, although seemingly ancient, are historical fact and a myriad of additional, more recent, historical examples could be made to emphasize the point that God is indeed actively involved in history. As we again consider the situation facing our country today, one can't help but wonder whether or not God will continue to bless us as he has in the past.

LORD, FORGIVE US FOR BEING A PROUD NATION. BEING A NATION THAT REJECTS YOU AND YOUR WILL HAS LED US TO BE SO PROUD THAT WE FEEL WE CAN DO EVERYTHING AND ANYTHING IN THE WORLD WITH OUR GREAT MILITARY FORCE. WE JUST DON'T SEEM TO LEARN THE LESSONS YOU HAVE GIVEN US IN THE PAST. OPEN THE HEARTS OF OUR PEOPLE AND ESPECIALLY OUR LEADERS TO YOUR WILL. HELP US TO LOOK TO YOU AS OUR SOURCE AND TO BECOME A HUMBLE NATION UNDER GOD. IN YOUR NAME WE PRAY. AMEN.

CHAPTER 16

Boasting, Overconfidence, and Conceit vs Humility

The word "boasting" has been used throughout this book, and now we need to more carefully examine the term and see what the Word says about it. Boasting is speaking exaggeratedly about oneself, or speaking pridefully in a manner which exuberates vanity. Since boaster is the term usually used to denote one who is proud, we need to remember that boasting is the outward expression of what we believe in our hearts. A person can be a proud person, be quiet about it, and still be in a state of sin. More often, however, we express outwardly what is within our hearts by using our tongue. In Chapter 3 the apostle James teaches us of the mightiness of the tongue and all the things it can do. One essential relevant teaching in Chapter 3 is found in verse 11. "Can both fresh water and salt water flow from the same spring?" The answer, of course, is no! The point James was making is that our tongue is the main way in which we communicate our inner thoughts to others. If we are continually boasting (with our tongue), we are indicating to others what is foremost in our heart-that is, we are thinking too much about ourselves, which would be the salty water. If we do not boast, we are more likely to be thinking inwardly about God, Jesus, or others-the fresh water! James is saying that since both salty and fresh water cannot come from the same spring, likewise, boasting and humility will not come from the same heart via the tongue. King David, in the 12th Psalm, gave a similar example of how the ungodly would use their tongue for deceit: "Everyone lies to his neighbor; their flattering lips speak with deception. May the Lord cut off all flattering lips and every boastful tongue that says, 'We will triumph with our tongues; we own our lips-who is our master?"

James adds more to his teaching on boasting in Chapter 4. "Now listen, you who say, 'Today or tomorrow we will go to this or that city, spend a year there, carry on business and make money.' Why, you do not even know what will happen tomorrow. What is your life? You are a mist that appears for a little while and then vanishes. Instead, you ought to say, 'if it is the Lord's will, we will live and do this or that.' As it is, you boast and brag. All such boasting is evil." (James 4:13-16) Here again, the tongue is expressing the thought that WE control our destiny, that WE will decide what and where we will be in the future. James knew that this kind of thinking left God out of the picture and was trying to explain that, if we are truly relying on God for everything we need in life, we should say, "If it's the Lord's will, we will . . ." We need to remember this today as we think and talk about our plans for the future, and it will reduce a great deal of anxiety in many of us! James may have remembered the saying of Solomon: "Do not boast about tomorrow, for you do not know what a day may bring forth." (Proverbs 27:1)

There are quite a few Psalms related to boasting. Throughout the Bible, men who reject God are often referred to as the "wicked". This is the case in many of the Psalms. In Psalm 12 we read: "In his arrogance the wicked man hunts down the weak, who are caught in the schemes he devises. He boasts of the cravings of his heart; he blesses the greedy and reviles the Lord. In his pride the wicked does not seek Him; in all his thoughts there is no room for God". (Psalm 10:2-4) From David we read: "Let me not be put to shame, O Lord, for I have cried out to you; but let the wicked be put to shame and lie silent in the grave. Let their lying lips be silenced, for with pride and contempt they speak arrogantly against the righteous." (Psalm 31:17-18) And in Psalm 94 we read: "Rise up, O Judge of the earth; pay back to the proud what they deserve. How long will the wicked, O Lord, how long will the wicked be jubilant? They pour out arrogant words; all the evildoers are full of boasting." (Psalm 94:2-4) In Psalm 52 David said: "Why do you boast of evil, you mighty man? Why do you boast all day long, you who are a disgrace in the eyes of God?" (Psalm 52:1) And, finally, in Psalm 17 we read: "They (the wicked) close up their callous hearts, and their mouths speak with arrogance." (Psalm 17:10)

Let's go back and pick out descriptive words found in these Psalms that indicate the personality of the "wicked" man, or in today's language, the "non-believer". Remember, these Psalms were written about men hundreds of years ago! These non-believers are arrogant, they hunt down the weak or dominate others, they devise schemes to con the innocent, they boast of their sensuous desires, they revile the Lord, they reject God, they lie, they speak with contempt about believers, they are jubilant in their conniving ways, they boast, they have callous hearts and speak with arrogance. WOW! That sounds exactly like some of the men we associate with every day! Could it be that the Bible is as relevant to us today as it was when the Psalmists wrote? Notice, particularly the last trait-they have callous hearts and speak with arrogance. Here, again, we have the tongue representing the heart, and in this case-a calloused heart that has rejected God. This is exactly the kind of person represented by many of the secular humanists today.

Paul was writing to the Corinthians about expelling the immoral from the body of believers and telling them that they were condoning conduct that even the pagans do not condone. A man in the body was having a sexual relationship with his father's wife and was proud of it! Not only was the sinner proud of the relationship, but so was the body! They were apparently even boasting about it! "Your boasting is not good. Don't you know that a little yeast works through the whole batch of dough?" (1 Corinthians 5:6) Once we members of the body begin to accept immoral conduct and begin to boast about it, it works like yeast; that is, gradually over the years the sin creeps into the body. Before long, everyone is doing it, and since it has become the norm, it is OK; it is no longer considered sin!

"Where, then, is boasting? It is excluded. On what principle? On that of observing the law? No, but on that of faith." (Romans 3:27) Although Paul was focusing on faith, he points out that boasting is (or should be) EXCLUDED from the life of the man of faith! If we are boasting, we are expressing our self-centered inner feelings of the heart through our lips. If our thoughts are self-centered, we are sinning. If our inner thoughts are on God, Jesus, the Holy Spirit, and others, then we will not be inclined to be boasting about ourselves. We are taught that if we must boast, we should boast in the Lord. It all boils down to whether we are self centered or Christ-centered.

Conceit is another reason for boasting. A person who is conceited is one who has an exaggerated opinion of his abilities or of his importance. Nearly everything we have explored about the nature of the proud person also describes the conceited person. He has an over-inflated image of his abilities. An important point to remember here is that God has given us all different abilities and different levels of proficiency in each. See if you can handle this statement: You

"Live in harmony with one another. Do not be proud,
but be willing to associate with people of low position.
Do not be conceited."
Romans 12:16

are indeed inferior in many respects to others! Boy, that is really tough for many to accept-especially for someone who is highly competitive. Modern psychology would never suggest telling a person they are inferior to anything or anyone! The fact is, since God has given us different gifts AND different levels of ability, we must accept whatever we have been given as a gift from God, and not be envious of what God has chosen to give to others. Therefore, even though we may have been gifted with a great ability, it is not of our doing-rather it is a gift from God. Why then should we be conceited? Rather, we should praise God for whatever GIFT we do have and learn to appreciate the fact that God has given different gifts of varying degrees to others and we should share their glory with them.

Being conceited is simply another way of saying "I have done great things". "Do you see a man wise in his own eyes? There is more hope for a fool than for him." (Proverbs 26:12) Because of conceit he thinks he is wise! If he was truly wise in a Godly way, could he possibly become conceited? No! He would know how unwise he really is and would be giving the credit for his wisdom to God instead of himself. Again, we must distinguish here the difference between doing the best with what God has given us, versus claiming all the credit for our accomplishments. As Christians, we have the responsibility to make an effort to do our best with what God has given us regardless of whether we are a genius in a certain area or are just "plain vanilla".

Paul was telling the Galatians about life led by the spirit, about acts of a sinful nature, and then, on the positive side, he indicated the fruits of the Spirit-led life. He then said: "Since we live by the Spirit, let us keep in step with the Spirit. Let us not become conceited, provoking and envying each other." (Galatians 5:25-26) Conceit and envy must have also been a problem with early Christians! We should, if we are living in the Spirit, be building one another up rather than being conceited, provoking or envying our brothers and sisters in Christ. Paul continues this teaching in the next Chapter. "If anyone thinks he is something when he is nothing, he deceives himself. Each one should test his actions. Then he can take pride in himself, without comparing himself to somebody else, for each one should carry his own load." (Galatians 6:3-5) Paul is saying, don't continually compare yourself with others, compare yourself with yourself and your own capabilities. Paul is actually rebuking conceit and gives a recipe whereby it can be avoided. We are to compare our achievements, not with the work of others, but with what our best should have been. When we do this, there can never be any cause for conceit. Paul adds one additional point to this subject in his letter to the Romans. "Live in harmony with one another. Do not be proud, but be willing to associate with people of low position. Do not be conceited." (Romans 12:16) With whom do you choose to be associated, people in high position, or positions of influence? Why? Because of what they might someday be able to do for you, or simply because it builds ego to be associated with someone important! That's man's way, not God's! The Bible tells us that we should be willing to associate with people of low position!

We are continually taught, as we are raised in our society, to develop confidence in ourselves. We could address this self-confidence in either a secular manner or in a spiritual manner. With a secular understanding, self-confidence would mean that one should have confidence in what THEY have, what THEY have accomplished, or what THEY can accomplish. In the context of spiritual understanding, one could develop self-confidence knowing that he/she was utilizing God's gifts in their lives to their maximum potential and be praising God for these abilities. The problem we are addressing more specifically here is OVER-confidence! Over-confidence implies full trust or over trust in that which one places his trust. To the man without God, placing an inordinate trust in one's own ability usually leads to conceit. As children of God, we cannot place too much trust in our creator, therefore, overconfidence should not be a problem for the Christian. "In Him and through faith in Him we may approach God with freedom and confidence." (Ephesians 3:12) "For you have been my hope. O Sovereign Lord, my confidence since my youth. From birth I have relied on you; you brought me forth from my mother's womb. I will ever praise you." (Psalm 71:5-6) "Should not your piety be your confidence?" (Job 4:6) We cannot be overconfident as Christians-it's impossible! The more confidence we place in our reliance on our creator, the closer is our walk with God. Also, in Job we read: ". . . the joy of the godless lasts but a moment. Though his pride reaches to the heavens and his head touches the clouds, he will perish forever, like his own dung." (Job 20:5-6) By being overconfident, the unbeliever may appear to be reaping great joy, but that joy is temporal. When the Christian places his confidence in the Lord, his joy is eternal.

Should we be surprised that godless men act with conceit, pride, and overconfidence? Not really! When Paul was writing to Timothy, he said: "But mark this: There will be terrible times in the last days. People will be lovers of themselves, lovers of money, boastful, proud, . . . conceited, . . . having a form of godliness but denying its power. Have nothing to do with them." (2 Timothy 3:1-4) Could that "form of godliness" be what we call secular humanism today? This author certainly believes so!

It is very clear that God's word teaches that conceit, pride, overconfidence, and boasting should not be traits of a Christian. "Haughty eyes and a proud heart, the lamp of the wicked, are sin." (Proverbs 21:4) What, then should we be like? That is a tough teaching! Yet, can't you see that if we were to learn to live that principle, it would be nearly impossible to become conceited! In his letter to the Colossians, Paul teaches: "Therefore, as God's chosen people, holy and dearly loved, clothe yourself with compassion, kindness, humility, gentleness and patience." (Colossians 3:12) In addition, Paul, in his letter to Titus, told Titus to remind the people to: ". . . show true humility toward all men." (Titus 3:2) James tells us to: "Humble yourselves before the Lord, and he will lift you up." (James 4:10)

These passages very clearly show us that we MUST MAKE EVERY EFFORT TO BE HUMBLE PEOPLE. Even though man's way is to be self-confident, we, as followers of Christ, must work at being humble. It's not easy, but we are commissioned to work at it as the attainment of a desirable human trait in God's eyes. And, if we do, there are many promises from God! Let's look at some of them. "Therefore, whoever humbles himself like this child is the greatest in the kingdom of heaven" (Matthew 18:4) "For whoever exalts himself will be humbled, and whoever humbles himself will be exalted" (Matthew 23:12) "If my people, who are called by my name, will humble themselves and pray and seek my face and turn from their wicked ways, then will I hear from heaven and will forgive their sin and will heal their land." (1 Chronicles 7:14) "He has performed mighty deeds with his arm; he has scattered those who are proud in their inmost thoughts. He has brought down rulers from their thrones but has lifted up the humble." (Luke 1:51) "He mocks proud mockers but gives grace to the humble." (Proverbs 3:34) "You save the humble but bring low those whose eyes are haughty." (Psalm 18:27)

Looking back at these teachings, which are from a variety of both New and Old Testament books, we can pick out the great promises God has for the humble. The humble will: be the greatest in the kingdom, will be exalted in the kingdom, will have their sins forgiven, will have their lands healed, will be lifted up, will be given abundant grace and will be saved! WOW! These are fantastic promises! Why haven't we looked into these before? Not only does God tell us that pride is a sin-He gives us a clear alternative and tells us of the great promises we will receive if we are humble! He also gives man the freedom to choose. We can choose to follow man's way; that is, be conceited and boast of our accomplishments, or we can choose to follow God's way and be humble servants.

HAVE MERCY ON US, O LORD, HAVE MERCY ON US, FOR WE HAVE ENDURED MUCH CONTEMPT. WE HAVE ENDURED MUCH RIDICULE FROM THE PROUD, MUCH CONTEMPT FROM THE ARROGANT. (PSALM 123:3-4) EVEN THOUGH WE RECEIVE THIS CONTEMPT FROM THE WORLD, WE THANK YOU LORD FOR YOUR SAVING GRACE, THAT GRACE THAT ENABLES US TO WITHSTAND THE CONTEMPT FROM THE PROUD IN THE WORLD. FATHER, WE KNOW WE HAVE A LONG WAY TO GO IN TRUSTING COMPLETELY IN YOU IN THIS AREA OF HUMILITY. HELP US TO ELIMINATE PERSONAL PRIDE FROM OUR LIVES AND REPLACE IT WITH TRUE HUMILITY. WE KNOW OF YOUR PROMISES, AND BY BECOMING HUMBLE SERVANTS WE CLAIM THOSE PROMISES. THANK YOU LORD FOR BEING OUR GOD. IN CHRIST'S NAME WE PRAY. AMEN.

CHAPTER 17

Praise

It should be clear to everyone by now that there is a great abundance of references and teachings about pride in the Bible—Old and New Testaments. Pride is a sin that was initiated and is perpetuated by Satan. It is often the dominating trait in a human personality. Pride is a sin in God's eyes; because, when we become prideful, we become self-centered, rather than Christ centered. As we grow up, become better "educated", acquire things, attain position, and so on, we are generally conditioned in our secular humanistic society to "pat ourselves on the back" for a job well done, rejecting the possibility that we have had help. We have been so conditioned to be independent and self-sufficient that we begin to believe that we have, in fact, done everything on our own; and, if we can do all these things on our own, who needs God! This is a false secular belief. From Genesis, Chapter 1, verse 1, through the book of Revelation, God has shown us of His works. God's works are so mighty compared to what mortal man can do that it is not even worth comparing the two. It is only by God's amazing grace that we are what we are and have what we have. By faith in Jesus Christ we can come to know God; and, when we choose to live according to God's way, we know He will provide us with EVERYTHING necessary for life. We then know that we don't have to prove anything about how good we are, because we know that we are His children-and that's the ultimate "somebody"!

When we become proud of the things we have accomplished in life, we usually seek the praise of others. Because society conditions us to be successful "in man's eyes", we look to man for approval or praise for what we do. That is man's way rather than God's way. "For they loved praise from men more than praise from God." (John 12:43) This teaching of Jesus' is so relevant to us today. Think about a routine day in your life. Whom are you trying to please most of the day? We try to please our boss, our mate, our children, etc., so that we will be well liked and receive praise from them. Seldom do we give proper attention to pleasing God and seeking His praise! Of course, by taking good care of our mates, children, and friends, we are doing God's work; but we have to continually remember who our ultimate source is and remember that all we do should be pleasing to Him—we should be seeking His praise, not man's. In fact, the Bible tells us that the real test for silver is the crucible and the furnace for gold, however we are told that the following is the test of man's worth: ". . . but man is tested by the praise he receives." (Proverbs 27:21) So, we are tested by how well we handle praise; but, is that received praise from man or God? Much has been taught and written about praise. Our brief discussion in this chapter simply examines praise as an antonym of pride.

Just what is praise? Praise, according to most modern dictionaries, means to laud, glorify, exalt, respect, show reverence for, to give tribute to, or to express admiration to someone. When we praise one another we are building up that person because of something they have done. Likewise, when we praise God we are building up God for something He has done (building up God in our own minds, that is!).

The phrases "Praise the Lord", or "Praise God" are used so glibly by many of us that we sometimes lose sight of the real meaning. When one gives praise, he/she is giving affirmation, or expressing approval for something well done. When we seek praise from man, we are seeking his affirmation or approval. When we seek praise from God, we are seeking His affirmation or approval. Which is more desirable for the Christian? Praise from God, of course. Certainly, it is nice to receive praise from man; that's "natural" and makes us feel good. However, when we receive praise, hopefully it will be deserved because we have been following the Word of God. When we obey God's Word, over a period of time, we experience a real overflowing of praise, joy, and thanksgiving, which is greater than anything we can ever hope to experience outside His Word. Not only should we seek to please God and, thereby, receive His praise, we should be continually praising God! This praise thing is a "two-way street". If we only work at receiving God's praise, we aren't giving anything. We must constantly give thanks and praise God for all the things He has done for us. There is a timeless secular proverb that says: "to get, you have to give". If we are to receive praise from God, we should be praising Him constantly, for this is what He wants us to do. We should worship God, not man! It is God's presence in us that makes us better than any other sinful man. That fact, and because of what Christ did for us on Calvary, should make us want to constantly praise Him.

Christ said: "How can you believe if you accept praise from one another, yet make no EFFORT (emphasis mine) to obtain the praise that comes from the only God?" (John 5:44) This statement really makes us think seriously about whether the proud person can really be a believer, if we assume his source of pride is himself, or praise from his fellow man! "For it is not the one who commends himself who is approved, but the one whom the Lord commends." (2

Corinthians 10:18) Paul was also trying to get this same point across in the book of Romans when he was teaching about the Jew that was seeking praise because he followed the Jewish law related to circumcision. "No, a man is a Jew if he is one inwardly; and circumcision is circumcision of the heart, by the Spirit, not by the written code. Such a man's praise is not from men, but from God." (Romans 2:29) God praises us for what is in our hearts-not for what we do outwardly that other men can see! "Therefore judge nothing before the appointed time; wait till the Lord comes. He will bring to light what is hidden in darkness and will expose the motives of men's hearts. At that time each will receive his praise from God." (1 Corinthians 4:5) It's very clear that on judgment day, God will either praise us or condemn us for what has been in our hearts, rather than for what man has seen us do in our lifetime.

This praise, to be received at judgment day is accompanied by a crown (blessing). We earlier defined praise as being lauded, paid tribute to, or glorified. When we are glorified we are crowned. "Who redeems your life from the pit and crowns you with love and compassion?" (Psalm 103:4) "Be faithful, even to the point of death, and I will give you the crown of life." (Revelation 2:10) "Blessed is the man who perseveres under trial, because when he has stood the test, he will receive the crown of life that God has promised to those who love him." (James 1:12) "And when the Chief Shepherd appears you will receive the crown of glory that will never fade away." (1 Peter 5:4) Wow! How could this knowledge help but make every man want to receive God's praise? By receiving God's praise, we will receive a crown of glory that will never fade away! That means we will be like "kings" for eternity! When we receive praise from man, we may get a "thanks", a few bucks more on our paychecks, and/or a temporary inflation of our ego!

There is no doubt about the consistency of the teachings

"Therefore judge nothing before the appointed time;
wait till the Lord comes. He will bring to light
what is hidden in darkness and will expose
the motives of men's hearts. At that time
each will receive his praise from God."
1 Corinthians 4:5

in the Bible, which say, if we do His will, we will receive God's praise. But receiving praise is only one side of the two-way street! We are also taught in the Bible to constantly thank and praise God for everything he has done for us and is doing for us in our lives.

There are two "classical" references in the Bible that are frequently used to show how Christians ought to live in relation to giving thanks or praising God. One is found in Ephesians and the other in 1 Thessalonians. They are both teachings of Paul and were included in letters written to believers in these two communities. They have been the basis on which several popular books have been written. "Speak to one another with psalms, hymns and spiritual songs. Sing and make music in your heart to the Lord, always giving thanks to God the Father for everything, in the name of our Lord Jesus Christ." (Ephesians 5:19) And, "Be joyful always; pray continually; give thanks in all circumstances, for this is God's will for you in Christ Jesus. (1 Thessalonians 5:16-18) The relevant words or phrases in these two passages are: give thanks . . . FOR EVERY-THING, and give thanks IN ALL CIRCUMSTANCES. According to some writers today, if we are to praise God for everything and in all things, then we cannot be selective and only praise God for good things. Their interpretation of these passages would lead one to believe that we should also praise God for all the horror in the world! This is not a particularly new thought. Some early church writers believed that we should even be thankful, and praise God for Hell, since it is a reminder for us to keep on the straight and narrow path. These writers would have us believe, then, that we should praise God for all the evil and suffering in the world (because God has a purpose in creating evil), as well as all the good in the world!

When we see a tragic automobile accident where there are several dead people lying around, do we say "praise

God"? When we see a close relative dying of cancer, do we say "praise God"? When we see children beaten to death by their parents, do we say "praise God"? When we see innocent children with birth defects that make them helpless cripples all their lives, do we say "praise God" for this? Did God plan or predetermine that these events would happen, as the theologian John Calvin suggests and, then, in the Bible tell us we should praise Him for these deeds? If, indeed, God knew beforehand that these horrible events were going to take place, and He let them happen, is not He also, then, responsible for them? Why did God create all things, including man, and say that it was very good (Genesis 1:30); change His mind in Genesis 6:5-7, and be grieved that He had made man, if He knew all along man would take the sinful path? If, in fact, God knew when He created him that man would choose the sinful way, why would He be grieved?

The problem we have here is that if God is good, we should praise all that God has created—goodness. If God is also responsible for evil, then we, indeed, should also praise Him for all the evil we see in the world today! Basic to this problem is the idea of predestination. Logically, we cannot reject predestination and accept foreknowledge. We must accept either both or neither. If man is truly the originator of his own choices, these choices cannot be known until they are made. Since God does not make all these choices for us He cannot be responsible for them, other than creating in us the ability to make a choice, or even know what they are until they are made. God is good because He chooses to be good. Evil exists because God has given us the free will to choose between good and evil; and man, in general, has chosen evil. Have you ever thought about doing something sinful, and then changed you mind? You probably have; and, if you have done it once, you have the power to resist it ANYTIME OR ALWAYS! But, do we (or man, in general) always choose good over evil? Unfortunately not! God created us with a free will. He gave us the ultimate gift of being able to choose between good and evil. This God given freedom carries with it the possibility of sin. If there is free choice, the possibility of good AND evil must exist. If it were any other way we would be mere robots, preprogrammed to do every act in life. Now, if God is not responsible for evil or suffering resulting from wrong choices, why should we praise God for those things? Maybe we should be praising Satan for those things, since he is the one who works on us continually to make evil choices-he is the father of lies! The original question we have been looking at is whether we should be praising God for "all things", or for "all good things". The important thing to realize here is that God is NOT responsible for evil, and the tragic events resulting from sinful choices of man individually (e.g., a man chooses to get drunk and kills a little child), or man corporately (e.g., using cancer causing agents to produce things that make our life temporarily more comfortable). God is not responsible; and, therefore, we need not praise Him for the result of that sinful conduct. HOWEVER, since God promises to be with us always, to share our joys as well as our sorrows, we can praise God with great confidence that he will be with us in ALL events of life-IF WE LOOK TO HIM. If we look to God in good times and bad times, and praise Him all the time, He will do great things in our lives and give us great comfort during the bad times.

Some time ago my wife developed a health problem. Within two weeks of the diagnosis, and as a result of many quick trips to doctors, she had brain surgery. There was no way in the world we could praise God for that physical problem in the brain! Yet, from the very beginning, we praised God for who He was, for His great healing power, for the near miraculous events that led to the possibility of the urgent surgery, for the Christian neurosurgeon who did the operation, for the successful operation, for the constant prayers of fellow Christians, for the compassion of our pastor, for the meals brought into our home for three weeks, for the visits of family and other loved ones, for the greater love my wife and I have for one another, even though we had been married for 35 years, ad infinitum! PRAISE GOD. PRAISE GOD. PRAISE GOD. God never has promised us that we would be spared from physical health problems, from accidents, from unjust punishment, from evil in the world, from suffering we do not understand, or even from death! BUT, He did promise that He would be with us ALWAYS-PRAISE GOD! ". . . Now is your time of grief, but I will see you again and you will rejoice, and no one will take away your joy." (John 16:22)

I love the response Daniel's three friends gave Nebuchadnezzar when he threatened to throw them into the furnace. "Shadrach, Meshach and Abednego replied to the king, 'O Nebuchadnezzar, we do not need to defend ourselves before you in this matter. If we are thrown into the blazing furnace, the God we serve is able to save us from it, and he will rescue us from your hand, O king. But EVEN IF HE DOES NOT, (emphasis mine!), we want you to know, O king, that we will not serve your gods or worship the image of gold you have set up." (Daniel 3:16-18) Even if God chose not to spare them, their faith was so great that they would not sacrifice their principles, even unto death.

Victor Frankle, in writing about his experiences in Nazi prison camps during World War II, said that the only reason he survived when others did not, was that regardless of what they did to him bodily, they could never destroy or take away his reliance on God. "My slanderers pursue me all day long; many are attacking me in their pride. When I am afraid, I will trust; I will not be afraid. What can mortal man do to me?" (Psalm 56:2-4)

There is no doubt about the fact that we should constantly praise God. He has, indeed, given us everything we need to live out our lives. "Sing joyfully to the Lord, you righteous; it is fitting for the upright to praise Him." (Psalm 33:1) "I will praise you, O Lord, among the nations; I will sing of you among the peoples." (Psalm 57:9) The Psalms are full of praise hymns. They remind us that if we are humble and sing praises to God all day long, we will not only be spared from being prideful, but we will also be a good witness to God's Word, to people, and to the nation as God's holy people.

"PRAISE BE TO THE GOD AND FATHER OF OUR LORD JESUS CHRIST, WHO HAS BLESSED US IN THE HEAVENLY REALMS WITH EVERY SPIRITUAL BLESSING IN CHRIST." (Ephesians 1:3) O GREAT GOD IN HEAVEN, HOW WE PRAISE YOU. YOU HAVE CREATED ALL THINGS, GIVEN US EVERYTHING WE NEED IN LIFE, SUSTAINED US IN TRYING TIMES, AND POURED OUT YOUR GRACE UPON US. WE KNOW WE ARE UNDESERVING OF YOUR LOVE, BUT THROUGH YOUR SON WE HAVE GAINED NEW LIFE. FORGIVE US FOR BEING PROUD PEOPLE GOD, AND GIVE US HUMBLE SPIRITS. HELP US TO REMEMBER WHERE OUR PRAISE SHOULD BE DIRECTED AND THAT WE SHOULD PRAISE YOU CONSTANTLY, NOT ONLY WITH OUR LIPS, BUT WITH OUR HEARTS. IN YOUR PRECIOUS SON'S NAME WE PRAY. AMEN

If, after reading this book, you have still not accepted Jesus Christ into your life, you can do it now. You can make your own prayer to God or you can repeat the following prayer, if you genuinely believe the words in your heart. But remember, if you do, your life will never be the same again and you will look at pride and praise in a completely different way.

GOD, MY LIFE HAS BEEN FILLED WITH PRIDE AND I HAVE LIVED A LIFE WHERE I HAVE FELT YOU WERE NOT NEEDED. I BELIEVED THAT I COULD MAKE IT THROUGH LIFE BY MYSELF. IN THE PROCESS I HAVE FAILED MANY TIMES AND I NOW REALIZE I CANNOT MAKE IT ON MY OWN. I RECOGNIZE THAT I HAVE SINNED MANY TIMES IN MANY WAYS, AND I ASK FOR YOUR FORGIVENESS FOR THOSE MANY SINS AND TRANSGRESSIONS I HAVE COMITTED AGAINST YOU. CHANGE MY LIFE GOD, MAKE ME A NEW CREATURE, COME INTO MY HEART LORD JESUS. IN THE NAME OF JESUS CHRIST I ASK YOU TO MAKE ME ONE OF YOUR CHILDREN. THANK YOU GOD AND HELP ME TO PRAISE YOUR NAME FOREVER. AMEN